Airbnb, Your Keys to Financial Freedom

Becoming an Airbnb Owner of Your Entrepreneurial Future

Donald Stanton

Table of Contents

Introduction

Financial freedom, or independence, is one of the first things people mention when you talk about life goals. It is one of the most rewarding accomplishments in life, knowing that you don't have to live in constant fear of your regular paycheck being late or being let go by your employer. The job market can be quite unpredictable, and even people with stable jobs have woken up one day and found themselves unemployed. Think back to the year 2020, and quite a number of people who had stable jobs and careers found themselves unable to fend for themselves as the COVID-19 pandemic ravaged economies all over the world.

It's quite interesting that while some people lived in fear of job loss, others welcomed it. They welcomed the break from the norm, the break from slaving every hour of their work day, pushing reports, sitting in meetings, and other rigors of the traditional job market. Most of those who welcomed this break had one thing in common, they had established a stable source of passive income.

See, the beauty of passive income is that your money works for you, and when you set up your money the right way, it really does a good job of that. While there are lots of passive income ideas and opportunities, we'll dwell on short-term rentals, specifically, Airbnb. Since the company has been around, hosts have earned billions on the platform. That's so much money that you shouldn't be missing out on, especially if you are thinking about your long-term financial goals.

As the popularity of Airbnb grows, so does the income-earning potential. More hosts join the platform every year, and so should you. One of the reasons for Airbnb's success is their revolutionary approach to short-term rentals. Before Airbnb, you'd have to book a hotel for your vacation. The problem with hotels is that they generally offer standardized services, more like template hosting services. While this generally works for their clientele, the rigid structured approach denies it the oomph that makes vacations memorable.

Airbnb challenged the hotel and hospitality industry by offering one thing hotels have struggled to offer over the years, a personal touch. When you check into an Airbnb, you are basically checking into someone's home. For the time that you'll be booked into their property, you'll use it as your own home. The allure of this homely feeling is one of the reasons why Airbnbs have become quite popular over the years.

Think about it for a moment, you could visit any country, check into an Airbnb and live in a house like yours. A comfortable bed, sofa, living room, catch up on your favorite Netflix shows on a 65" TV just like you normally do at home. You can also step out and buy stuff from the local grocery store to prepare your meals just the way you do at home without being restricted to the local cuisine, or having to make do with whatever specials hotels prepare on that day. These are some of the perks of checking into an Airbnb over hotels. Indeed, you might still enjoy the freedom to do all these things in some hotels, but the convenience comes at an additional cost. Airbnb, on the other hand, gives you the benefit of living your life on your own terms. Other than the fact that you're in a new location, everything else remains unchanged. This means that if you're on a strict diet, you can keep it up—you don't have to worry about whether the hotel will prepare your meals the right way, or use the right ingredients according to your meal regimen.

These are some of the benefits guests derive from Airbnb. People love convenience, and that's where you come in as a host. Provide comfort and convenience and you'll be smiling all the way to the bank. As far as value proposition is concerned, comfort and convenience are two of the most important things people seek on vacations. People are willing to pay more for the assurance of these two factors. A private beachfront property for your vacation beats spending your vacation with hundreds of other hotel guests, competing for attention from the overworked and often underpaid staff.

Airbnb is about you.

Unlike other passive income opportunities, hosting on Airbnb gives you flexibility and convenience. You can do it part-time to suit your lifestyle or the demands of your career. You can also scale up your short-term rentals and run a full-time business. You can invest by buying your property, or if you can't afford that, you can consider rental arbitrage. You can also host shared spaces, where you invite guests to live with you and share your life with them. The fact is that there are many ways to make money through Airbnb. You just need to figure out which one you are comfortable with, and invest in it.

It's pretty obvious that Airbnb has some serious investment opportunities that could turn your life around. We won't dwell on that in this book. Instead, we'll show you how to identify these opportunities and capitalize on them. At the end of this book, you'll have answers to common first-time investor questions like how to plan your Airbnb, choosing the right location for your investment, whether the short-term rental business model is profitable or not, and how to turn your humble beginnings into a steady and reliable profit-making business.

You literally have the keys to your financial freedom in your hands once you set up your first listing on Airbnb. Stop reading about other people's Airbnb success stories, and let people get inspired by your story. Traditionally, real estate has always been considered a safe financial investment, especially if you are thinking long-term. This is because the real estate industry has withstood the test of time. From pandemics to wars, natural disasters, and global financial crises, the real estate sector always bounces back. This resilience is what makes real estate a stable investment.

On a grander scale, if you've ever been interested in the real estate market, Airbnb is your easiest way in. You're not just investing in an amazing listing, you are using Airbnb to lay the foundation of your entrepreneurial future.

Chapter 1: What Is Airbnb?

Airbnb, Uber, Netflix, Amazon...

These are some of the biggest digital brands in the world today. They are so big that their success or business models have spearheaded transformations in their respective industries. They are not just seen as the epitome of success—global brands, learning institutions, and researchers have often used their business models for benchmarking.

While these brands are synonymous with success in the modern digital world, the underlying factor in their business models, and which makes them the behemoths they are today, is their transformative impact in their industries. They sparked a revolution and continue to champion changes in different dimensions.

Airbnb changed the hotel industry so much that many hotels, the world over, list their rooms on the platform. In essence, Airbnb is pretty much the largest hotel chain in the world, yet the company doesn't actually have an establishment where guests can physically check in. With millions of listings, Airbnb managed to give the likes of Accor, Marriott International, InterContinental Hotels Group, and Hilton Worldwide a run for their money, and from the look of things, there's no relenting in this battle. But, how did we get here?

According to Airbnb, there's at least two million people being hosted in other people's properties every night (Wood, 2017). You can bet that there's not a single hotel chain in the world that hits those numbers a night. Apart from this, the Airbnb website lists the following amazing statistics as of March 31, 2022:

- more than six million active listings all over the world

- active listings in hundreds of towns and cities all over the world, spread out in more than 220 countries and regions

- more than a billion guest arrivals thanks to over four million hosts since inception

- hosts have earned more than $180 billion

With such impressive statistics, it's hard to imagine that this company, worth billions today, was once just a couple of guys renting air mattresses in their San Francisco apartment to earn a few extra bucks, and to basically make rent! Well, that's the story of Airbnb co-founders, Brian Chesky, Joe Gebbia, and Nathan Blecharczyk.

Airbnb started in 2007 as nothing but two hosts welcoming guests to their apartment. Despite the lucrative business that it has become, the founders had their fair share of struggles, just like most startups do. They initially got three air mattresses and set them up in their loft anticipating guests who were attending a design conference in the city.

One of the challenges the trio faced was giving their idea the perfect launch. In fact, by 2008, they had failed at three attempts to launch the company. Even worse, Chesky happened to be one of only two customers in their third attempt at The South by Southwest (SXSW) Film Festival in 2008. Later in the year, they redesigned their concept and set out to pitch to investors. The new concept was a platform where users only needed to click three times on their website to book a stay. The reasoning behind this was that anything more than three clicks was an unnecessarily complex process.

Unfortunately, investors weren't buying this idea either. Seven of the fifteen investors they pitched to ignored them, while the other eight formally rejected their pitch. The company was already burning holes deep in their pockets around the time Denver, CO played host to the DNC. The DNC presented a unique opportunity to try the only thing that had worked for them so far, hosting strangers. Learning from the design conference in San Francisco, they knew Denver didn't have the capacity to host all the guests attending the DNC. Around this time, the election wave was sweeping across the country, so they decided to capitalize on it.

The version of the Airbnb website that existed at the time wasn't bringing in any income, so they jumped onto the Obama wave. They rebranded cereal boxes with Cap'n McCains and Obama O's, selling them to guests at $40 each. The guest influx also presented a huge marketing opportunity for the startup. Each cereal box included information about their startup, and a limited-edition number. This was one of their smartest moves so far, earning around $30,000 to fund their Airbnb project.

Eventually, someone took notice. Venture capitalist (VC) Paul Graham realized their potential and welcomed the trio to Y Combinator, one of the most lucrative startup accelerators in the country. Y Combinator has launched more than 3,000 companies, including Coinbase, Cruise, DoorDash, Dropbox, Quora, PagerDuty, Reddit, Stripe, and Twitch (Sarath, 2022). Airbnb was finally in the right company and getting attention from the right people...or so they thought. Investors still rejected their concept.

2009 was a good year. Sequoia Capital invested close to $600,000 in the company, helping them finally stop fighting for scraps and start growing their business. It would take them four years from the San Francisco air mattress host experience to record a million nights spent by guests through their platform. By this time, Airbnb was live in 89 countries (Mohamed, 2020). Bolder and armed with lessons from previous failures, the trio went back to SXSW and this time, in 2011, they took home the Break-Out Mobile App Award (Elliot-McCrea, 2011).

They had venture capitalists and other investors right where they wanted them—excited and interested in their product. Silicon Valley VCs invested more than $100 million into the company, pushing its valuation to $1 billion. Airbnb had achieved a rare feat, earning the coveted Silicon Valley unicorn status, extremely rare and highly valued (Agence France-Presse, 2018).

Belong Anywhere

Airbnb had been on a steady and impressive growth trajectory since Sequoia Capital's investment. Buoyed by a $1 billion valuation, the company had all it needed to expand its reach. However, the rapid growth meant that it was only a matter of when, not if, problems would arise. With a business model built around hosting strangers and welcoming them into your home, hosts would soon start experiencing some of the harrowing issues that hoteliers have complained about for years.

Difficult guests, guests trashing their space, guests throwing parties, or guests that are too noisy they become a nuisance for the neighborhood, are just some of the issues that hosts had to deal with. Airbnb's solution was AirCover, a policy covering damage worth up to $1 million for hosts (Airbnb, 2022).

Problematic guests were becoming a bother everywhere, and authorities at different levels had to step in. For example, hosts started receiving eviction notices from their homeowners associations (HOA), while others were fined for running sublets against the terms of their lease agreements. Clearly, while Airbnb had mostly evolved to be the product that shook up the hotel industry, the need for regulation was even more apparent.

Cities all over the world became apprehensive about the Airbnb business model. Even worse, there were calls to ban or limit Airbnb in different parts of the world. Airbnb was having problems in New York and San Francisco. Apathy was ruining their brand and something had to be done.

Airbnb rebranded in 2014, complete with a new logo, the Bélo, to symbolize the sense of belonging the company was aiming for. They started collecting and remitting hotel taxes where applicable. This was aimed at strengthening their promise of belonging to a community. They didn't just want to have people hosting guests, they wanted to be part of the communities within which hosts and guests interact. Belong Anywhere was informed by the fact that the vast Airbnb community was so big, and growing exponentially, that the community had already outgrown the Airbnb brand (Atkin, 2019; Marion, 2021).

Most people limit their knowledge or understanding of Airbnb to the concept of short-term rentals. However, the team's vision had evolved. Airbnb wasn't just about renting houses, it was about homes. Home is where you belong, and Airbnb was encouraging guests and hosts to understand that they could feel at home anywhere in the world.

Can Airbnb Make You Money?

The short answer is yes! Hosts are already earning lots of money from Airbnb, so if you ever had doubts, cast them aside and look at how you can get in on this business and start earning yourself. As far as the vacation rentals industry is concerned, Airbnb is one of the smartest innovations of our time. Both hosts and guests stand a fair chance of benefiting from using this platform.

Guests love it because they have a plethora of vacation options. At the same time, hosts enjoy it because it gives them access to an entire world of customers. While it's true that you can make a lot of money from Airbnb, there's no guarantee that it will be a walk in the park. To be fair, there are many hosts who set out on a mission to earn through Airbnb, but for different reasons, called it quits.

Whenever you mention the possibility of earning through an innovative business idea, people generally flock to it, hoping that it will be a relatively easy feat to achieve. Unfortunately, they soon realize that there's a bit more work involved than they had imagined, and they grow cold feet.

To join the growing list of hosts who have amazing success stories from Airbnb, you must be prepared to do the work and earn your money the smart way. Airbnb does pay off. A few things that will work to your advantage include the fact that there's a wide range of property types that Airbnb accepts as habitable for their customers. You could start anywhere from renting out that spare room in your house, or talk to your landlord about letting you rent out your entire space as a furnished apartment. You might even earn by offering your couch for someone to sleep on. That's how easy it is to get started on your journey to financial freedom through Airbnb.

Now, let's talk some hard facts. While the thought of getting some money from renting your property might be alluring, not everyone is cut out for hosting. Are you comfortable with strangers coming and going from your property all the time? For someone who's quite particular about their living spaces, you have to think deeply about this and make peace with it.

Next, since guests come and go at their pleasure, you'll have to be hands-on about cleaning and maintenance. Review your schedule to see if you can slot in time for this. If not, you'll have to consider outsourcing some of the property management tasks from the very beginning. Hosting is more than just handing over your apartment keys to guests, it's a commitment to effective communication, marketing your property online, and being prepared to deal with mishaps and last-minute changes to your schedule. Think occupational hazards and this will make sense.

Since there are many properties in the same neighborhood, what's so unique about yours that makes it stand out from everyone else? Why should a guest skip all the other properties and book yours?

As far as profitability is concerned, you must always think about value creation or value addition. Granted, your house has a sleeping area, kitchen items, and so on—these are basics, the bare minimums of any vacation rental property. If that's all you have to your name, you might limit your profit potential. The secret to winning on Airbnb is to make your property different. Add some perks to entice guests. Offer a little bit more than what your guests are paying for.

The key is to make the homestay experience as memorable for your guest as possible. Who doesn't like free breakfast? If you can, why not offer your guest free breakfast? If they are new to town, perhaps you can create time in your schedule and show them around, help them explore the greatness of your neighborhood. There's so much you can think of which will serve this purpose. It might cost you a few dollars here and there, but this is an investment into creating an amazing reputation. It will eventually pay off, especially when you read the glowing reviews from your guests. The idea here is to create the kind of listing that makes your guests realize they are getting so much more value than what they paid for. Do that, and your calendar will always be booked.

Cost of Setting up an Airbnb

Fully aware of the fact that you can earn a decent income from Airbnb, the next step is to figure out the real cost of setting up this business. Like we mentioned earlier, try not to get so fascinated by the potential profits that you ignore the realities of doing business. This, like every other business, has a number of operational costs that you must plan for. Let's go through some of them below.

Service Fees

This is what Airbnb needs to run an operation so smoothly that you can earn a steady income from their platform. The service fees levied by Airbnb help them offer important services like customer support. Service fees can be charged either as a fee to the host or a split fee between the host and guests.

For split fees, the service fee is split between the host and guest, so everyone pays a portion of it. On the other hand, the host fee will see you pay on average three percent of the booking fee to Airbnb. This, however, will also vary according to certain requirements. For example, if you are an Airbnb Plus host, you will pay more (Tom, 2022).

Airbnb Plus is a premium service for top-quality homes. Hosts in this category generally have a knack for glowing reviews, while their attention to detail is another feature that makes their properties stand out from the rest. Airbnb actually conducts in-person inspections on such properties to verify their authenticity and design, ensuring that only the best of the best enjoy the benefits of their premium service (Ditaranto, 2020).

You might also pay more in service charges if your cancellation policies are very strict.

Taxes

As more hosts join the Airbnb platform, local authorities realize the need to widen their tax bracket by taxing various services on the Airbnb platform. If your property is in an area under which VAT and other tax policies apply, it is your obligation to pay taxes as required.

Tax rules vary from one place to another, so it's common to find some areas being taxed higher than others. If you do your math and realize that your taxes are higher, it makes sense to use the host-only service charge. This way, you don't pass the tax burden down to your guests, which might scare them away. The same applies if your cleaning or any other costs are high. It makes sense to find a way to absorb such costs on your end, and let customers enjoy a seamless, cost-effective stay.

Chapter 2: Planning My Airbnb

What do you want to get out of this business? This is perhaps one of the most important questions that many hosts forget to ask themselves. When it comes to planning for your Airbnb, there's so much more to it than thinking about the money. Indeed, money is important in the long run, but you must also have something else pushing you.

Case in point, Airbnb has it as their mission to belong anywhere (Execs In The Know, 2022). Everyone who signs up on Airbnb either as a host or a guest will buy into this mission somehow. A clear mission gives you a sense of direction, reminding you why you are doing this. This is particularly important during those times when the market is in a slump, and you are hardly making any money.

Your mission is your guiding principle, and in a way, sets the bare minimum you can accept from guests or from the Airbnb ecosystem. If you ever get to a point where you feel your mission no longer aligns with the Airbnb model, you can simply call it quits and move on to other things without any hard feelings.

The mission statement will be crucial in this planning process, because everything you do will be guided by it. Here are some things that you should think about:

Your Motivations

What drives you? In a business that caters to guests at a personal level, you will come across easy and difficult guests alike. Some guests are so bad, you might rethink your investment in Airbnb and probably want to walk away altogether. Being motivated can help you rise above this, remain steadfast, and continue pursuing your goals.

Your Core Values

What do you believe in? Interacting with people can be challenging. People share different beliefs about a lot of things. Whether you intend to host on a shared platform or leave the entire space to your guests, your approach to hosting on Airbnb will be largely influenced by your beliefs. If there are things you don't like, you certainly won't be comfortable with your guests doing the same in your house. You must strongly consider this because it will ultimately affect your relationship or interaction with guests.

Your Preferred Mode of Operation

How do you intend to run your business? There's so much involved in running an Airbnb that you might not be able to do it all on your own. With that in mind, think of how much help you can get, and plan for it from the very beginning. While outsourcing is a good idea, it costs money and you might not really need to outsource so much from the start.

Read about what other beginners did, their experience with outsourcing, and learn from it. It might actually be more motivating to push yourself if possible and handle most of the tasks on your own. This makes it easier to get a clearer perspective of your income potential in the business.

The points raised above are important, not just when running an Airbnb, but in any other business venture you might get into. Remember, a good plan is one that's driven by a clear mission. The fruits of your labor will be even sweeter in the long run because you can look back to where you started, and appreciate how far you have come.

The Secret Weapon—Location!

Having established your mission, let's get down to planning. The first thing you want to get right in the real estate business is location, and the same applies to Airbnb. Location will be crucial to your profitability and long-term success. Of all the advantages your property might have, location is one of the most important which serves as its biggest asset.

Take a moment and think like a guest...why would you want to book this property?

Many hosts fail because they don't consider this. They think about their business from a host's perspective, and this robs them of the opportunity to consider the value they are adding in a guest's life. More often, guests complain that the property was too far, or something else about the location. Hosts hardly care about such complaints because at the end of the day, some other guests appreciate the property and were fine with it.

As far as location is concerned, you should be thinking about a needs assessment approach for your guests. You have a target audience in mind. What kind of activities would they like? How do they generally travel? What amenities would they be comfortable with? These are some simple questions that can set you in the right direction. Now ask yourself if your intended location meets these demands and you'll see why location is important.

A common mistake hosts make, especially those who live in the same neighborhood, is to assume that guests will like and enjoy the same facilities and amenities you do. The longer you live in a neighborhood, the more subjective the location becomes for you. Therefore, your opinion on distance to certain places will mostly be biased, and if a guest complains about how far it is to get to some place, you'll probably brush it off.

Guests have expectations. Whether implied or apparent, they expect them to be met. Ease of access, ambience, connectivity, accuracy on the map, convenience, the neighborhood, the community, and even your next-door neighbor, are some of the things that guests hope are true based on the information you have online. At times, some of these factors are implied. For example, if you say the property is located in a nice, quiet, homely neighborhood within a gated community, guests could book hoping to find a homely family setting. You can imagine their surprise if it turns out you have one of those neighbors who throws parties with loud music all the time. There certainly is nothing homely about that. Such things might be out of your control, but your guests won't extend you the benefit of the doubt on that. To someone who was hoping for a peaceful vacation with their family, you lied, and that will certainly go into their reviews.

Value judgements play a huge role in our decision-making process. Guests will judge your location based on factors you know nothing about, but are dear to them, especially when they consider the price they pay to use your property. It's important to understand, therefore, that the decisions your guests make about the location you choose will not always have anything to do with the physical location on the map. In some cases, their decisions will be influenced by your description, or even their instinct. This is why location is one of the most important, yet difficult, factors to handle when selecting your Airbnb. While you can only speak for yourself on the value proposition of a location, you must also take into consideration so many unknowns that your guests care about.

Since there's only so much you can do about guest choices, focus on what you can influence. For starters, ensure your location is as accurate as possible. Describe the route if necessary, indicating all the necessary landmarks.

I can't stress this enough, but invest a lot of effort into understanding the needs of your target audience. People's tastes and preferences change all the time, so this might not be an easy one. However, you can have a rough idea by keeping up with trends. This will help you figure out the kind of places your target audience spends most of their time, then narrow down your location options within a proximate distance from such.

Ultimately, even if you realize that your target audience prefers to be as close as possible to night clubs and other noisy entertainment joints, this doesn't mean your property should be in a noisy place. At the end of the day, people want to come to a nice quiet place after a long night out.

Next, you can avoid bad reviews by ensuring your location description meets some customer requirements, or at least, can help them make a decision before confirming the booking. For example, some people claim they own beachfront properties yet in reality, the property is nowhere close to the sand. This is the kind of deceptive description that customers will not appreciate. To make your property even more appealing, you can indicate some of the notable facilities, buildings, or businesses in close proximity to the residence. This could inspire confidence in your guests, especially if they notice something they like.

To make your work easier, Airbnb allows you the following options when setting your property location:

- Specific location: In this case, the Airbnb map will display a pin on the nearest street. Note that this will not indicate the exact location of your property. However, you can simply drag the pin on the map to the correct location.

- General location: This shows the general area where your property is located. General locations usually give a half-mile proximity accuracy.

By default, your property will be set to a general location. You can, however, customize your map for more specificity by choosing the specific location setting. Once you do that, you can provide more information to make the description as precise as possible so your guests have an easier time finding the property. As a rule of thumb, the easier it is for your guest to get to your property, the higher your chances of setting off on the right note.

Profitability Assessment

Building on our discussion from above, let's shed more light on a location factor that's of great importance to you—profitability. Despite your interest in making it easier for guests to find your property, a location will only be relevant to you if it is profitable in the long run. It serves no purpose to appeal to guests but end up with a property in a location that doesn't meet your investment objectives. Remember that at the end of the day, you are working towards financial freedom.

You can find a beautiful property with the kind of space that appeals to most guests, giving you the advantage of widening your target audience. However, even with the space and amenities, if the property is in an undesirable neighborhood, you'll have trouble getting return customers or referrals. The fact that you have no influence on the location means that you either get it right from the beginning or make a big mistake that will cost you dearly.

So, as far as profitability assessment is concerned, what makes one location better than the others? For this section, it will be in your best interest to think like a realtor. Here are some crucial things you should consider when making your choice:

Crime Rate

Well, crime is one of those things that you never want to think about, but you have to. When we talk about the desirability of a location, crime is one of the factors that contributes immensely to that status. The fact that you probably won't be spending a lot of time on the property means that you need a place that's so secure you don't have to worry about burglaries simply because no one is home.

Whether you live in the residence or not, the safety of your guests must always come first. Most guests are new to your location, so they know nothing about the security situation in that neighborhood. It would be quite unfortunate for guests to suffer a security incident while on your property. Besides, security issues are unnecessary attention you probably don't want from the authorities.

In most cases, hosts who have security incidents tend to close down and move to a different location after that. Now think about all the hard work and investment you put into looking for this location and setting it up. Imagine the resources, the time, the connections with cleaners, handypersons, and so on. All that will go to waste.

It is relatively easy to learn about the crime rates in a neighborhood these days. Local crime reports are posted online all the time. You can also follow the local security agencies on social media to learn more about the kind of crimes common in that area or the security measures taken to reduce or prevent crime altogether. Where crime is concerned, you'd rather be prepared than sorry, especially since this will directly affect your income.

Schools

Now, schools are a subjective issue. This is because even though you might not be targeting families with school-going kids, proximity to schools might still affect your profitability. Generally, schools tend to influence the desirability of a location in the real estate market. Properties are more expensive in locations with quality schools than other areas. Therefore, the presence of certain schools in your neighborhood will almost automatically influence the kind of rates you charge guests.

Another issue that you will realize about schools, is that they can tell you so much about the quality of life in a neighborhood. Some school districts deliver more value appreciation to property owners than others, which also translates to higher demand and better-quality guests. Guests generally book their stay in areas that they are comfortable with.

Assuming that you are primarily targeting families, especially those with school-going children, proximity to good schools will mean that, by extension, the location has access to other facilities and amenities like playgrounds, recreational parks, and lots of fun activities for children. The more facilities your guests can access with their families, the higher the chances that they'll book to stay for longer. Families tend to prefer having easier access to facilities as it is cost-effective in the long run.

Transport and Public Amenities

Ease of access is of utmost importance to your guests. Earlier in this chapter, we mentioned how proximity can be subjective, especially if you live in the neighborhood. Apart from accuracy in your listing description, you simply need to ensure that you choose a location where your guests can access the property at all times.

What transport options are available? Can they use public transport late at night, or do they have to use ride-hailing apps like Uber? What about the amenities and facilities your guests might require? How close is the property to grocery stores and restaurants? What about entertainment and shopping outlets?

Easy access to the subway station or bus stop might be convenient for your guests, but at the same time, no one wants to book a property close to all that noise. Therefore, you must find a careful balance that accords your guests convenience and the pleasure of comfort.

Your Neighbors

There isn't much you can do about your neighbors. You can't choose them, you can't change them, and you can't also kick them out. They might probably be thinking the same thing about you too. Despite these challenges, a good neighbor might actually be good for your profitability.

Your guests seek a peaceful residence, one where they can relax, have a good time, and that lives up to their expectations of a memorable stay. If your neighbors are the noisy kind who throw parties all the time, or play loud music or any other kind of nuisance, you can be sure this will reflect in your guest reviews. One or two reviews with the same experience is a pattern that will make a lot of guests avoid your listing altogether.

Peaceful coexistence is important in every society. If you have good neighbors, you will naturally feel the need to vet your guests better so that you can equally ensure your neighbors don't ever have to complain about unruly guests on your property. Good neighbors, especially those that you have a good relationship with, can also be your second line of defense on security matters when you have guests. If they notice something odd about your guest, they can alert you, so you act promptly and prevent unforeseen losses.

Note that when it comes to good neighborliness, you can only get as much as you give. If you have good neighbors, be good to them, and your guests will have an awesome time on your property.

Future Value Appreciation

In the real estate business, it's always wise to invest in locations that have good potential for value appreciation. Future appreciation potential means that there's something unique about that neighborhood that makes it attractive to property owners, tenants, and other stakeholders in the wider real estate market.

For your short-term rental business, this is good news because you can comfortably increase your listing values over time to match the property demand. A desirable neighborhood attracts investors. Investors create more value by putting the land to use. This eventually increases the demand in that neighborhood, which is good for your business.

Structural and Aesthetic Appeal

The Airbnb business is big on aesthetic appeal. This is one area where you cannot afford to compromise. It gets difficult because unless you own the property, there's not much you can do about its architecture. In some cases, you might also be restricted in your freedom to upgrade the aesthetics of the property. Some landlords simply don't need you making any changes to their property and are fine with it as it is.

Take your time and study the property before you invest in it. Get a property inspector to give you a professional assessment of the property. The condition of a house tells so much about its age. While some guests appreciate old houses for their history, that's a very small niche that probably won't be profitable for you at the beginning. Most guests prefer modern houses.

From a business point of view, old houses can be quite expensive to maintain. The upkeep costs will eat into your income, so there's really no point of investing your money and time in old properties. For your first investment, it will be wise to find properties whose maintenance and upkeep costs won't bleed you dry.

Budget

How much does it cost to run that house? This is one of the most important profitability factors that many beginners ignore. It's easy to get caught up in the allure of nightly prices that you forget the real expense items in the house. You can make so much money from your short-term rental, but as long as you don't have the expenditure under control, it might not be as profitable as you have imagined.

Before you invest in an Airbnb, understand that there will be days when you won't have any income. During these days, the property must still be kept in a habitable condition, just in case you secure a last-minute booking. The utility bills must be paid on time, your cleaning team must be paid their dues on time, and any other expenses must be paid as well.

As you search for properties that you can use for this business, consider the average cost of running that house. Weigh this against the potential income and see whether it fits your budget. Interestingly enough, you might have a clearer picture of the expense items than the potential income because you have no certainty that guests will come to your property, and for how long. If you have to keep digging into your savings account to prop up your Airbnb, you clearly invested in the wrong property.

Before you commit to any property, study the market and find out as much as you can about the costs of running that house. This will make it easier to determine whether you are working within a reasonable budget or not.

Insurance

Finally, consider the insurance demands of that house. As much as you will enjoy host protection under Airbnb, you must understand that Airbnb's protection is not an insurance cover. You need insurance for your business. The cost of insurance depends on a lot of factors, from proximity to water to other factors unique to that neighborhood.

Find out what the current or previous owners of that house used to pay in insurance, then start planning. Remember that since you are running a short-term rental, you will host strangers all the time. Your property is more of a business now than a normal household, so discuss your options with your insurer to get a clearer picture of what to anticipate, then plan accordingly.

As you can see above, there's so much you should consider when assessing the profitability of your Airbnb. From location-specific factors to factors unique to your business or even your own business goals and objectives. The secret is to plan. Effective planning helps you stay ahead of the competition. By planning well for unforeseen circumstances, you'll have an easier time running a profitable business.

The Right Business Structure

Now that you have everything figured out, you need a solid business plan. A business plan maps out the finite details of your business, which could also make your work easier if you ever seek financing from a bank. To create your business plan, you must first figure out a suitable business structure.

You have already done your research, you understand the market, have engaged different professionals, and are certain that this will be a good move. Up to this point, your business is more of a concept. To move from concept to reality, you have to establish your business as a legal entity. This basically means registering a business.

Whether your local administration requires it or not, it's always wise to run your Airbnb under a registered business name. This is important because registering the business makes it a separate legal entity from you. This means that while you run the business, you are not the business. Therefore, by registration, the business assumes its own identity as legally conferred to a person. It can enter into legal contracts on its own accord, without you.

While there are various reasons why business registration is important, perhaps the most valuable to you at the moment is liability. By registration, your business becomes a legal person. This means that it can be sued. In the event of any damage, all liability will be on the business, not you. Therefore, if one of your guests or your neighbors is ever to be compensated, they will be compensated on the basis of the accounts and assets held by your business. Your personal effects will not be involved in such matters. Therefore, if the worst comes to pass, you might lose the business, but you will not lose your personal effects. It is for such protections that you need to register your business. Here are the main business structures under which you can register your Airbnb:

Sole Proprietorship

By default, all hosts operate as sole proprietors. A sole proprietor is non-registered. As an unincorporated business, the sole proprietor (business owner) makes all the decisions of the business. The problem with this model is that there exists no distinction between the owner and the business.

As a sole proprietor, you will earn all the profits of the business. At the same time, you are liable for all the losses, debts, and any other liabilities that might befall the business. This is the risk we mentioned earlier. If the worst ever comes to pass, you lose not just the business, but any of your personal effects that might be attached to the liabilities associated with your business.

Without the legal protections of your business as a separate entity, you are always at risk of losing everything. This, certainly, isn't the kind of business structure a smart investor should adopt.

Partnership

A partnership is a business structure where two or more people come together with a common objective. In this case, together with your partners, you pool resources with the common objective of running an Airbnb business.

There are different kinds of partnerships, but the basic structure does not involve the formation of a legal business entity. In this case, you just come together with your friends, pool some money and set about finding a property to use as an Airbnb. Like sole proprietorships, this approach means that you (the partners) bear full responsibility for the business.

Profits and losses are often shared under an agreed-upon structure. In most cases, this is usually done according to the share of each partner's contribution to the business. Therefore, if you contributed 20% of the total amount invested, that becomes the value of your ownership. In this case, you will only be entitled to 20% of the profits earned or losses incurred in the business.

Limited Liability Company (LLC)

An LLC is one of the most secure business structures. From the name, you can tell your liability is limited. This means that unlike sole proprietorships and partnerships, the business is responsible for its losses. You will not be held personally liable for any liabilities or debts incurred by your business.

Seeing that you are running a business that caters to strangers at a personal level, this is an ideal structure because where strangers and personal needs are involved, there's always a chance that things might not go according to plan. Besides, guests are at liberty to use your property. Unfortunately, some guests take these liberties too far.

The three structures above are the easiest to work with, especially for beginners. They are, however, not the only structures available. As your business grows, your needs might evolve, making it necessary to consider other options. S Corporations and C Corporations might be your next step. These structures, however, are considerably complex for the simplicity that defines the Airbnb business model.

Taking a lesson from Airbnb's workbook, this platform is all about simplicity. They take away some of the institutional bottlenecks that are common in the hotel industry, and make it easier for hosts and guests to engage. That's the approach you should take when choosing your business structure. Simple, efficient, and effective. At the end of the day, you should remember that this is a business, and for that matter, your profitability will always come first. You are investing in your future, so choose a business structure that aligns with that plan.

Chapter 3: Comparative Review of Airbnb's Business Model

One of the first things to consider before investing in any business opportunity is the profit potential, and the same applies to Airbnb. For a company whose business model basically takes the battle to hotels, some of which have been around for decades, it's in your best interest to understand whether Airbnb is not just profitable, but how it compares to other companies using the same model. This assessment is necessary because apart from competing for guests with other hosts on Airbnb, you'll also be competing against established hotel chains and other short-term rental companies for the same customers. To get more insight into Airbnb's profitability position, we'll take a comparative approach in this chapter, analyzing various factors that can help you make an informed decision ahead of your investment.

Airbnb's Competitive Edge Over Hotels

Airbnb has been on a steady growth trajectory, with more guests opting for their personalized service model over the rigid structure provided by hotels. Thus, the growth profile doesn't come as a surprise. While this growth can be attributed to various factors, including flexibility during the COVID-19 pandemic, we will emphasize three key reasons unique to Airbnb below, which have convincingly spurred the company's growth, and more importantly, made their business model more appealing to guests over hotels (Tatevosian, 2021):

Encourage Longer Stays

Think about it for a moment, if you needed to travel somewhere for an extended period of time, say a few weeks or months, which would you choose between a hotel and an Airbnb? Airbnb wins this round. Granted, you'd probably want to stay in a hotel the first few days, but after some time, the homely appeal on Airbnb will win you over.

Of course, hotels have some unique benefits, but if you look at the overall experience, you'd be better off in an Airbnb. While hotels might offer convenience, comfort might not be guaranteed. Besides, you still have to contend with sharing the space and facilities with other guests, their quirks included.

You'll generally have to pay more for laundry, meals, drinks, and so on, not forgetting the fact that most hotels have strict meal schedules. On the other hand, you can simply select the facilities you need in an Airbnb for your long-term stay and check into a property that meets all your needs so you don't have to pay extra for things like laundry, which you can do on your own. In most cases, hosts who have strict guest policies can relax their rules for long-term guests, allowing you to host guests from time to time, but with proper and prior communication (Tatevosian, 2021).

Group Dynamics

Group travelers get more value in Airbnb than hotels. Think about it, you generally have to reserve or book several rooms for your group at hotels, which is quite expensive. On the other hand, all you have to do on Airbnb is find a home that can accommodate everyone comfortably.

It gets even better, because the home setup gives you the benefit of privacy, so you don't have to share facilities and experiences, like mealtimes or a swimming pool, with strangers. This closeness makes your trip more exciting. You live like a family, prepare your meals together, hire a chef or order in and eat together, play together, and do so many other things together that you wouldn't normally be able to do in a hotel setting.

While some hotels can move things around to accommodate group travelers under such dynamics, such conveniences come at a cost, making group travel more expensive. Airbnb, therefore, is more than just a financially viable option for groups, but also presents a wholesome, refreshing, and better experience for groups than hotels (Tatevosian, 2021).

Not Your Typical Destination

Airbnb's location choices move away from the traditional hotel concept. Most hotels choose high-traffic locations, particularly locations that attract a lot of tourists. With this in mind, you can understand why big hotel chains prefer locations like New York,

London, and Paris. You can never go wrong with such locations, given the level of tourist activity.

While this model works for hotels, you must also understand that such locations don't come cheap. Everything from the cost of construction to the cost of living is at a premium, which hotels conveniently pass down to their customers.

Hotels tend to shy away from locations that lack this appeal, and looking at the cost factor in their business model, it makes sense. However, this also means that there's a large population that's underrepresented and underserved by hotels, and this is where Airbnb comes in (Tatevosian, 2021).

You can set up an Airbnb anywhere, subject to the local laws, rules, and regulations, of course. Through Airbnb, you can capitalize on such locations, serving a wide range of guest needs from those who need an entire home to those who need a shared room or even your garage.

It gets even better because while Airbnb is spreading their wings in areas that a typical hotel chain would consider unusual, they still ferociously compete for guests in the big cities and other locations favored by hotels.

From the three factors above, it's clear that Airbnb is not just taking the war to hotels, but actually winning over guests by virtue of the convenience and ability to comfortably accommodate various traveler needs, a trend that will persist into the future.

Airbnb vs. Competing Platforms

Hotels are not the only competition you'll be going up against once you sign up on Airbnb. There are many other players in the market, and judging by the success Airbnb has enjoyed so far, you can expect more competition in this space in the future. Notable competitors in the industry include Expedia Group's VRBO, Booking.com, TripAdvisor, 9Flats, and Flipkey. Each of these competitors have unique business models, so for the purpose of this comparative discussion, we'll focus on VRBO, whose business model is almost similar to Airbnb, and discuss the other platforms later in this chapter.

VRBO isn't another new kid on the block. Originally dubbed Vacation Rentals by Owner, the company has been around since 1995, even though the present owners, Expedia Group, bought it in 2015 from HomeAway, who coincidentally bought it in 2006. From the owner profiles, it's clear to see that VRBO is backed by a wealth of experience in the vacation industry (Lardinois, 2015).

VRBO's unique selling point is that unlike their popular competitor Airbnb, they only offer vacation homes. This means that guests have the entire apartment, condo, or house to themselves. This is different from Airbnb, which supports otherwise unconventional options like shared spaces, camp sites, and hotel rooms.

Once again, we see Airbnb enjoying a strategic advantage of both worlds, just as we saw in the location preference over hotels. If you are looking for an entire space to yourself, you can get listings on both VRBO and Airbnb. On the other hand, if you are looking for shared spaces, Airbnb is your go-to place. Airbnb has everything you need, from rural to urban centers, beachfronts to cabins in the woods, shared or entire apartments to yourself.

It's safe to say that one of Airbnb's biggest advantages is their unique ability to set foot in different markets, serving the diverse needs of guests and hosts all over the world. From a hosting perspective, it's always wise to learn more about the competition, especially their unique advantages over your preferred hosting platform. This puts you in a better position to gain more insight on guests from different platforms and leverage this diversity to increase your bookings.

Despite being considered an industry leader in the vacation and short-term rentals industry, boasting millions of users and bookings, Airbnb does not have a monopoly in the industry. If anything, the company's business model is currently being fought in different jurisdictions and has even been mentioned as one of the contributors to the housing crisis (Barker, 2022).

Besides, alongside platforms like Uber and Netflix, Airbnb's disruptive impact transformed the vacation rentals industry. The magnitude of Airbnb's success is proof of the industry's receptiveness to technological advancement and further disruption. Who knows what will happen in the next five or ten years? One thing that's certain, however, is that you need to position your short-term rental business strategically to capitalize on technological, legislative, or any other advancements that disrupt the industry in the future.

Airbnb, VRBO, or any of the other platforms that exist or might come up in the future, you can't go wrong. List your property wherever you can. Even better, sync your booking calendar and use a good property management app to streamline your listing management. This will smoothen your management experience, so you don't have to keep switching from one platform to another, while also helping you avoid double bookings and other booking conflicts.

Whether VRBO and other platforms are similar to Airbnb will depend on their product offering, their target audience, and their unique proposition. To be fair, every new business that joins this space in the future will use Airbnb for benchmarking by virtue of its success, popularity, and global brand recognition.

From an investor's perspective, it's always wise to explore different options for greater visibility across multiple platforms. This strategy can help you achieve your business goals faster. Besides, there's no rule against cross-listing your property on multiple platforms. As a rule of thumb, always go where you can find your target audience.

Alternatives to Airbnb

Vacation rentals is an age-old industry that has seen many players come and go over the years. That Airbnb is currently one of the most popular companies in this industry doesn't mean they enjoy a monopoly. If anything, Airbnb's rapid success has stirred competition in the industry, with other companies rushing to innovate or reinvent their business models with unique value propositions, hoping to not only compete against Airbnb, but also increase their market share.

To be precise, there are billions of dollars up for grabs in this market every year, hence the stiff competition among brands. Here are some of the notable companies other than VRBO, that are giving Airbnb a run for their money:

Booking.com

Booking.com started out as an aggregator platform for guests seeking short-term accommodation in hotels and other residences. They have since diversified into the vacation rentals sector, with their tremendous growth attributed to massive investment in marketing and advertising all over the world (PhotoAdKing, 2022).

As far as private accommodation is concerned, the company has maintained its reputation as one of the reliable platforms for guests seeking accommodation in holiday apartment-style or hotel residences. Airbnb, on the other hand, is mostly about individuals and small-time investors trying to maximize the income-earning potential of their properties.

To boost their competitiveness, both companies are actively invested in providing innovative solutions for customers at different points in their vacation journey. From tailor-made experiences to flights, car rentals, and restaurant reservations, there's so much to look forward to as these companies try to outdo each other.

Expedia Group

Expedia Group's market share has grown through strategic subsidiary acquisitions over the years, expanding their reach and making them a serious competitor to Airbnb. To counter Airbnb's global brand visibility, Expedia Group tends to focus on acquiring subsidiaries that enjoy significant regional popularity, making it easier for the company to enjoy grassroots-level growth (Wealth Insights, 2019).

It's worth noting that this is almost similar to Airbnb's approach of setting up in locations that hotels generally tend to avoid. Thus, Expedia Group goes after country or region-clustered brands, and perhaps in the future, we might see all the subsidiaries identified under the conglomerate's brand.

That being said, inspired by their mission to *belong anywhere*, Airbnb continues to penetrate the same regional markets as Expedia Group, so this, like we saw with Booking.com, is another battlefront worth your attention.

FlipKey

From their humble beginnings as a house-swapping platform in 2007, FlipKey has grown over the years, diversifying into the highly competitive vacation rentals market following their acquisition by Tripadvisor in 2008. By 2016, the company had listed properties in more than 170 countries, allowing them to compete against industry behemoths like Booking.com and Airbnb (PRWeb, 2014).

Their business model has since evolved, pursuing common industry goals like providing a wholesome travel experience for guests, including restaurant recommendations, flight bookings, car rentals, and suggestions for local tour activities.

FlipKey's relationship with Tripadvisor is one of their strongest selling points, leveraging millions of traveler reviews on Tripadvisor to boost their performance. This is an advantage that even Airbnb cannot match. The beauty of traveler reviews is that they provide more insight into travel destinations, making it easier for guests to make more informed decisions when planning their holidays.

Within a short span of time, Airbnb has managed to position their brand as an industry leader despite competition from older and more established brands, reinvigorating an industry that for a long time, had hosts wielding most of the power. Airbnb's entry into the business didn't just transform the industry, it forced brands to rethink their business strategies to customer-centric models. From the tales of Superhosts and many other investors who have made a fortune off Airbnb, it's clear that putting the needs of guests first is one of the most important ways to succeed. This applies not only to Airbnb, but also when listing your property with competing brands.

Ultimately, the vacation rentals industry is still growing, and Airbnb's rejuvenation probably isn't the last step in the evolution of this industry. Whether Airbnb swallows up all the competitors and becomes a monopoly is yet to be seen. One thing that's certain, however, is that Airbnb will be at the forefront in championing changes that bring forth innovative advancements in this industry.

Older, Experienced Competitors

Once you set foot in the vacation rentals business, it's best to keep exploring your options. As much as Airbnb will be at the center of your business model, your desire for profitability and creating a sustainable and scalable business means that you must equally cast your gaze beyond Airbnb. As a property manager, you have to explore all options available, and one way to go about this is to study the market and understand the value inherent in older, seasoned companies that have been there before Airbnb.

It's important to note that despite Airbnb's prominence in the vacation rentals industry, there are a number of established companies that existed before Airbnb who have similarly grown their business over the years. These companies have loyal customers, some who swear by them and would never consider Airbnb.

You must also be aware that Airbnb's success comes with a number of challenges, especially where legislation is concerned. It's no secret that Airbnb's business model is currently being fought in different jurisdictions across the world (Neubauer, 2019). With this in mind, it doesn't hurt to consider diversifying your business into other platforms and explore other niches. As a business owner, your emphasis should be profitability and growing your brand, a brand that will outlive Airbnb and other platforms you intend to use. Here are some of the seasoned competitors you should consider for your business:

HomeToGo

This is one of the biggest search engines in the world, giving users access to millions of listings from hundreds of platforms like Airbnb. This aggregation platform makes work easier for guests by allowing them to make side-by-side price comparisons from different platforms. This feature makes it an ideal platform for travelers on a budget.

It's important to note that while HomeToGo might not be a direct competitor to the Airbnb marketplace by virtue of being a search engine, the fact that it gives customers access to many other marketplaces makes it a platform you should consider as a host. Don't just limit yourself to Airbnb. Instead, go the extra mile, and get more exposure with HomeToGo and other platforms that we'll discuss herein.

Google

Well, since HomeToGo is on this list, it only makes sense that the mother of all search engines makes a grand entry too. Google's capacity has, over the years, grown beyond its search engine functionalities. If you are keen, you'll realize that Google frequently drops suggestions on Google Maps results or if you make any travel-related search. This is why we cannot discount Google's influence in property visibility within the vacation rentals industry.

Google has a number of partners in the vacation rentals industry, so listing your property with such companies allows you to leverage their relationship to your advantage. This way, your property will probably show up in search results relevant to your location. Harnessing Google's power of visibility gives you front-row access to millions of potential customers. It gets even better—Google is free!

The beauty of using Google as a search engine is that it doesn't limit your potential customers to Airbnb, it shows them listings from other platforms too, which is a good thing for the purpose of growing your audience and business.

Tripadvisor

As far as vacation rental reviews are concerned, most travelers consider Tripadvisor as their go-to platform. Used by hundreds of millions of users every month, Tripadvisor connects visitors to different types of accommodations while also linking them up with other complimentary services that could add more value to their trip.

With more than 20 years in the industry, Tripadvisor is a trusted platform for everything from planning your trip, booking, and enjoying the entire experience. Travelers can find reviews on anything from vacation rentals to tourist attractions, restaurants, accommodation services, and local activities.

Like other online travel agencies, Tripadvisor brings together more than just vacation rentals. While Airbnb is limited to property listings and experiences, Tripadvisor gives you access to so much more. Therefore, it makes sense to consider listing your property on Tripadvisor and any other platform that can get you more exposure.

In retrospect, there are lots of other metasearch engines like Agoda and tourism companies like TUI Villas that offer stiff competition to Airbnb's business model. You also have Plum Guide, which primarily offers luxury vacation rentals. As you can see above, Airbnb faces stiff competition from different angles, and it's even more complicated when you consider the aggregation capabilities of search engines in this battle. From an investor's point of view, you need brand visibility, so you should list with as many platforms as possible. At the end of the day, the popularity of Airbnb will mean nothing to you if you are not getting guests to your property, or if you are not getting as much traffic as everyone else.

It's not easy to pick one company and claim it as the best alternative to Airbnb, not even those that have been in the business for decades. This is because while Airbnb mostly offers access to vacation rentals, competitors in this list offer that and so much more. Indeed, Airbnb remains one of the most recognizable brands in the world for vacation rentals. However, each platform boasts unique advantages and disadvantages in line with their core business model. This is why your best move is to list wherever you can, or where you believe you'll get the most value for your money.

Long-Term Sustainability

Will Airbnb be sustainable over the long run?

Well, the short answer is yes. This is a global brand that's basically taken on hotels and other players in the short-term rentals sector, forcing most of them to rethink or reinvent their business models. Airbnb championed innovation in the industry at such an unprecedented scale that most people would never have imagined possible.

Essentially, if you look at the fundamentals of short-term rentals, there's not much of a difference between checking into a hotel or checking into an Airbnb. You are still checking into a property with check-in and check-out rules. You enjoy your freedom to live in and use the property the same way you would live in your own home. You get to shop for food and drinks at the local market just like you would at home, without worrying about being restricted to a hotel's food or drinks, and so on.

Airbnb takes the hotel model and slaps on a whole lot of convenience, and in an industry that caters to guests at a personal level, convenience goes a long way. While this works, there's more to the long-term sustainability of the Airbnb model than convenience. Here are some reasons why Airbnb is sustainable over the long run and why it is one of the best investment decisions you can make:

Opportunities Everywhere

Unlike hotels that traditionally thrive in big cities and urban centers, the Airbnb model can be implemented anywhere. This means that even in a rural setting, you could still earn a decent income from your short-term rental.

Maximize Utility

One of the best things about investing in an Airbnb is you'll make the most use of assets and utilities that you already own. Your guests use items that are already in the house, like furniture and utensils. This is even more productive for shared spaces. This is an ideal situation for investment because you don't have to keep buying new items for guests all the time.

Apart from items within the house, Airbnb also helps you make the most use of space in your home that would have otherwise been empty. This is particularly applicable over the weekends and during the holidays.

Personal Touch

As we've mentioned before, the hotel industry is built on providing accommodation at a personal level. Airbnb exemplifies this personal touch. Guests experience everything from the hosting experience to the culture exchange at a more personal level at Airbnbs than in hotels. The fact that someone can live with you, in your home, and share meals and your culture, adds a touch of authenticity to Airbnb experiences that you probably won't get in hotel chains. At best, hotels simply usher you into the hands of their business partners in the industry for sightseeing and other local attractions. Most of these are often overcrowded anyway so you might not get as personal an experience as you'd get from an Airbnb host.

The Brand

Airbnb is one of the most recognizable brands in the world as far as the sharing economy is concerned. From their value proposition to the global positioning, there's so much room for immediate and future growth for hosts, which is one of the main reasons behind their sustainability. The fact that hosts keep discovering niche markets to serve within the wider Airbnb community further strengthens this concept.

Selling Experiences

One thing that sets Airbnb apart from hotels is that while hotels mostly sell the brand name, Airbnb relies on hosts to sell experiences. Selling experiences gives guests the benefit of breaking away from the monotony of brand concepts, allowing guests a new experience with every host they interact with.

In pursuit of new experiences, many guests have since moved on from hotels, and would rather book their holidays through Airbnb. This is purely on the fact that Airbnb hosts generally offer a more authentic and personal experience than they could get from hotels, hence Airbnb's growing list of loyal customers.

Besides, the intimate interaction between guests and hosts offers a unique experience that can never be replicated in hotels. More often, when you check into a hotel, you are left alone in your space, and only interact with room service and other hotel support staff on a need basis. Hotel stays, to be honest, are lonely. When you book an Airbnb, however, your host becomes a part of your experience in whichever capacity you can gain access to them. We can see this concept in the origin story of Airbnb, when founders Gebbia and Chesky hosted the first guests in their apartment. This personal touch is something that will always be a selling point for Airbnb.

Ultimately, Airbnb's long-term sustainability comes from the seamless integration of trust, internal culture, feedback loops between hosts, guests, and the Airbnb team (Mohammed, 2020). Even if someone were to copy the model today, the most they could achieve is a replica of their website. As far as the internal workings of the Airbnb ecosystem is concerned, the company enjoys strategic advantages that might not be easily replicated elsewhere, because each of the factors relevant to the brand's sustainability have been cultured into the Airbnb project from its formative years, with systematic tweaks for greater efficiency over the years.

Chapter 4: Airbnb vs. Long-Term Rentals

Would you rather list your property on short-term rentals like Airbnb or rent it out as a long-term rental? Each of these options carries its fair share of pros and cons. As an investor, your best move is to put your money where you can get the best returns. In the previous chapter, we outlined some reasons why investing in Airbnb is sustainable over the long run. At the same time, it's also evident that long-term rentals have existed long before Airbnb, and many people still prefer this model. So, the most important question is that while each of these models are profitable, which is the better of the two, and more importantly, which is the most suitable for your investment motive?

Airbnb has experienced tremendous growth over the years, and alongside this growth, the raging debate of whether investing in Airbnb is better than investing in long-term rentals. Granted, everyone has their own opinion on this, some out of experience, and others out of choice. One thing that we can all agree on is that in a way, Airbnb has transformed the travel and vacation landscape. Whether you choose to invest in an Airbnb or a long-term rental is ultimately a personal choice, guided by your investment goals and objectives. In this chapter, we will try to elaborate on the differences between these two models, and hopefully at the end of it all, you can review your plans in line with your investment vision, and choose a model that works for you.

Fundamental Differences Between Short and Long-Term Rentals

Whether it's your spare room or second home, the thought of an extra source of income has never been more enticing. Unless you've been living under a behemoth of a rock, times have been hard for a while, long before the COVID-19 pandemic, which only made things worse. Since then, the pursuit of a steady stream of passive income has seen many people consider making money from renting out the extra space in their households, or their second homes.

While this is a brilliant idea, there are many decisions you'll have to make down the line, which ultimately influence the profit potential of your venture. One of these is whether to lease your property as a short-term or long-term rental. Each of these options comes with unique benefits and challenges, so you have to assess the market, and choose one that delivers the most value.

Naturally, you'd want to compare each of these options on the basis of their pros and cons. Before you do that, however, it's wise to understand the difference between these two investment models. After all, one of the most important lessons in any investment is to ensure you put your money in something you fully understand.

There's so much more to the differences between short-term and long-term rentals than the duration a guest stays in the property. It is from these fundamental differences that you will eventually consider the pros and cons to determine the best option considering your investment objectives.

Short-Term Rentals

Also known as vacation rentals, short-term rentals are furnished spaces available to guests who generally use them for a given period, usually between a few nights and a month, or no more than six months. This classification, however, is not cast in stone, as the duration generally depends on the neighborhood and market dynamics. The target market for short-term rentals are mostly guests who would usually stay in hotels. However, instead of being confined to typical hotel accommodations, they opt for better services, amenities, bigger space, and more privacy in short-term rentals.

Naturally, short-term rentals would be ideal for guests seeking temporary accommodation when visiting friends or family, relocating to a new town, waiting to close on a home sale, renovating or flipping their primary house, tourists, or business travelers.

While short-term rentals offer promising returns, you should also be aware of the legal implications of investing in different neighborhoods or cities. You might also have to adhere to local HOA rules, which could impede the potential profitability of your venture.

Assuming all factors align in your favor, including legal and administrative costs, short-term rentals have proven to be quite profitable, and with the right management approaches, you can easily set up a steady stream of passive income.

Long-Term Rentals

Like short-term rentals, the definition of long-term rentals depends on the location. For example, while some states consider long-term rentals to be longer than 180 days, others consider stays exceeding 30 days to be long-term. Even so, most long-term rental contract terms are based on lease agreements exceeding one year.

As an investor, if you opt for long-term rentals, you must ensure you have the right target audience in mind. long-term rentals are generally ideal for individuals seeking some form of stability in life, for example individuals or families that recently moved to a new location. Moving can be quite expensive, not mentioning the risk of damage or loss. As a result, most people try to avoid moving frequently, and would rather find a decent residence, move in and not have to worry about moving out for a while.

From a guest or tenant's point of view, long-term rentals are useful for planning purposes. Since the contract terms are agreed upon beforehand, it's easy to plan financially, not just for the rent, but also for other expenses like utility bills. With this in mind, long-term rentals are relatively easier to plan for, especially when working on a budget, because the rental expense doesn't vary every few weeks or months unlike short-term rentals. On your part as an investor, long-term rentals generally attract lower administrative costs compared to short-term rentals. This is because of the considerably lower guest turnover ratio.

Flexible Rentals

Even though our discussion is solely on long-term rentals and short-term rentals, it doesn't hurt to mention flexible rentals, which are a hybrid of the two. Flexible rentals allow you to enjoy the best of both worlds. By leveraging their unique advantages where possible, you try to maximize the income-earning potential of your property by aiming for optimal occupancy rates.

Let's say your long-term rental is vacant around the time your city is hosting a big event with lots of tourists and guests expected. At this point, it could be smart to set your property up for short-term rentals, so you capitalize on the spontaneous demand.

Note, however, that while flexible rentals come with the benefits of both worlds, you will also have to deal with their drawbacks in equal measure. To protect your investment, you must have a contingency plan in place for both long and short-term rental guests.

Pros and Cons

Given the choice of short or long-term rentals, it would be wise to weigh their pros and cons to understand which of the two would be a suitable investment. In this section, we will compare the two investment models by looking at different factors that might be important to your investment agenda.

Income Potential

Short-term rentals generally are an excellent opportunity to earn some extra cash. The fact that you can create a flexible schedule and your own rates gives you sufficient room to maneuver, putting you in control of your income. Besides, since you don't need to commit to a lease agreement, you can always quit when you feel your needs are met.

On the other hand, long-term rentals lack the kind of flexibility outlined above. Your tenants will mostly be tied down to lease agreements of at least a year. While this gives you an income guarantee, you cannot increase the rent until the lease agreement expires or is due for renewal. The nature of the lease will also see you miss out on demand-driven profit opportunities like the summer vacations, since your property is tied up in the lease.

Management Experience

You'll commit more time to managing your short-term rentals than long-term rentals, especially if you manage it on your own. You can mitigate against this, however, by using different property management programs, or hiring a property management company to look after your house.

While managing long-term rentals can be considerably more time-consuming than short-term rentals, it is relatively easier because you get involved once in a while. Management mostly involves repairs, maintenance, or any other concern that your tenant might have. If you have hands-on tenants who are conscious about their living spaces, they might even handle most of the work on their own, and only inform you for accounting purposes. This means that you don't have to run around looking for contractors.

Set-up Costs

Short-term rentals are generally more expensive to set up. You have to put aside a considerable amount to furnish the property tastefully and competitively, lest you miss out on bookings. Apart from furnishings, you must also stock up on linens, toiletries, and other inventories to ensure the space can comfortably host a guest at any time.

Long-term rentals don't require as much costs as outlined above. If anything, you don't need to think about inventory, linen, or toiletries. You might not even need to prepare the space for tenants beyond simple cleaning. Once your tenant moves in, they are responsible for cleaning and in some cases, maintenance, until the day they move out.

Scheduling Concerns

As we mentioned earlier, short-term rentals give you the benefit of flexibility. You can rent the property out whenever you want to, and for as long as you need to. This makes it convenient in that you can always list your property when you need to supplement your income, or capitalize on holidays and profit from the demand.

Your inability to adjust property values while a lease agreement is in effect means that you cannot enjoy the same scheduling benefits as short-term rentals if you own a long-term rental property. The only way to make a lot of money is by having lots of tenants.

Factors to Consider Ahead of Your Investment

Our discussion on pros and cons above should be an eye-opener. Before investing your money, you should review various factors that will affect your business, because these generally influence the pros and cons. Getting your property from the conceptualization stage to the point where you earn a steady income could take time. Knowledge of some crucial factors, however, can help you streamline this process and have a relatively easier experience than most beginners do. Let's quickly review some of the factors you should be aware of below.

Investment Objectives

Assuming that everything goes according to plan, what do you intend to get out of this? One of the biggest mistakes that many people make in this business is going in because other people are doing it. Granted, you might make some money while at it, but without a clear ideology behind your investment, you could lose that money faster than you made it.

Before investing in anything, it's always wise to map out clear goals and objectives. Where do you see yourself in five, seven, or ten years? What do you intend to do with the property once you attain your targets? If you succeed in this venture, how does that success affect or influence your personal life? These are some of the crucial questions you must understand before you start dreaming up returns from your investment.

When setting objectives for your investment, use clear and measurable metrics. As much as you might have a sentimental attachment to the property, focus on the numbers. Sentiment won't bring in the money. Think about your vision for the property and create a roadmap to help you achieve it.

Hire Professionals

Once you start welcoming guests to your property, you'll soon realize the importance of working with professionals. You need cleaners, handypersons, electricians, and so on. These are the people who will ensure your listing is always ready for the next guest. As soon as one guest checks out, get your cleaners on site to prepare the property.

You might not need people like plumbers and electricians all the time, but when the need arises, you can be certain it's almost always an emergency. With this in mind, you should look for professionals with years of experience in the industry. More importantly, get people who can be available on demand, because you can never predict when your guest will need their help.

Other professionals that will be useful to your cause include a real estate agent who has in-depth knowledge of the neighborhood and the local market. In the rentals business, location is usually one of the key determinants of profitability. You want to invest not just in a prime location, but also in a location with a considerable influx of your target audience.

Market Research

Study the competition, always. This is also something a good real estate agent can help you with, given their knowledge of the market. Market research is diverse and will include anything from your competitors to the general market dynamics. Some useful data you can get from this include the average occupancy rates for similar properties, general operating and administrative expenses, HOA regulations, seasonality, and average nightly rates for similar properties.

This information will help you plan, not just for the competition, but also to get a realistic view of your investment. It will help you realize whether your assessment is naively optimistic, so you can adjust accordingly and adopt a more realistic approach.

Laws and Regulations

The market for short-term rentals has come under intense scrutiny over the years, especially given the rapid growth that Airbnb has enjoyed globally. While growth is a good thing, it has not been without its challenges. From rowdy tenants to criminal elements, there have been lots of complaints about nuisance guests, prompting relevant authorities to institute stricter rules and regulations to bring some sanity back to neighborhoods.

To be precise, there are some communities where short-term rentals are not allowed, while others allow them but under stringent conditions that might not be feasible for your profit objectives. Even in locations where short-term rentals are allowed, your property owner might be against it. In some areas, you might be barred by the local HOA. These are some of the factors you should consider because they will influence your profitability in one way or another.

Management Reality Check

Property management will play a significant role in determining your success or failure. The ease or difficulty of doing business will always come down to your property management approach. Most beginners assume that once they have a listing ready, everything else is seamless, and that's where they go wrong. As soon as you welcome your first guest, you realize that this might not be a walk in the park like you might have imagined.

To succeed in this venture, you must think of it as a professionally-run business. You'll be interacting with guests from diverse cultures with unique needs, preferences, and demands, and you have to cater to them in the best way possible. Let's go over some simple tips that could help you smooth your management process and make your life a bit easier.

Another Source of Income

You need another source of income. Even if you are lucky enough to welcome a guest within a few hours of listing your property, you'll still need a backup plan. Renting out your extra space is definitely a good source of income. However, it should not be something you rely on.

Let's say you have mortgage payments due every month. You should still be able to keep up with the payment schedule whether you have guests or not. Thus, if you don't have another source of income, you'll need to have an emergency savings account in case things don't work out. Remember that as a business venture, you are taking on an unknown amount of risk, and there's no guarantee that you'll get guests or tenants.

Lease Agreements

Your lease agreement is as much a binding contract as any other. It's a pity that many beginners never consider the weighty contractual obligations when leasing their property. Assuming that you intend to earn from your property through rental arbitrage, the original contract with your landlord might make or break your business. Go over it with your attorney to ensure you are not contravening the terms of that agreement by setting up a short-term rental.

This is an important consideration because many people have either lost their income or been kicked out of the premises by their landlords or under the recommendations of the resident HOA. While it might seem unfair, you should also understand that you are bound by the terms of the lease agreement. Before setting up a short-term rental, it's always wise to discuss this with your landlord, and from there, review the terms of your contract to ensure you are both on the same page.

Background Checks

For a business that primarily involves welcoming strangers into your property, you certainly cannot underestimate the need for background checks. It's relatively easier with platforms like Airbnb because they collect some personal information about guests, which can be useful if there's ever a need to follow up on the guest during or after their stay. For some properties, you can also request a security deposit before guests check into your property.

For long-term rentals, however, most of the hard work involved in background checks is up to you. As many landlords will tell you, people aren't always who they portray themselves to be. Have an elaborate interview or screening process in place before you hand over the keys to your house to someone. Ask for references and check their credit scores. It's in your best interest to have tenants who will not just be pleasant to work with but can also afford to live in your house.

Ultimately, you should realize that you are not just managing your property, you are also managing people. From your guests to the team of professionals working for you, everyone has a role to play in your success. This is where things can get complicated. At the end of the day, this is an investment into your financial future, so you must ensure that everyone you interact with by virtue of the property treats your investment with the respect and diligence it deserves. To summarize this section, the ease or difficulty of doing business will depend on your management approach, hence it is a matter of perspective. While some people might find it difficult, others might be having the time of their lives, and vice-versa.

From our discussions above, it's clear that whether you choose the Airbnb model or long-term rentals, you'll have some tough choices to make. While each model has some lucrative benefits, it would be foolish to ignore the possible pitfalls you might encounter down the line. As an astute investor, it's always wise to plan from the worst possible scenario than maintain a naively optimistic outlook. This borrows from the accounting principle of prudence, that you should never overestimate the amount of revenues recognized, or underestimate the expenses incurred. At the end of the day, this is a relationship business, and when catering to guest needs at a personal level, your profitability in the industry will always be at the mercy of their dynamic tastes and preferences.

Before opting for either short or long-term rentals, you must conduct due diligence and perform in-depth research. More importantly, you have to understand the guiding rules and regulations that govern each business model within your local jurisdiction. The best option isn't just one that works for you financially, but also one that will legally do so for years to come.

In all fairness, there's no perfect answer as to the better of the two. This is true because what you might consider a hindrance might be an advantage to you in a few months or years down the line. It might also be the key selling point for other investors in the same market, so ultimately, the pros and cons are not cast in stone, and at best, should be reviewed as a matter of perspective.

Holding all factors constant as an investor, you will be mostly guided by the earnings potential of whichever option you choose. Long-term rentals offer more stability in the market and by locking down tenants on longer contracts, you have the income certainty. On the other hand, short-term rentals allow you the benefit of flexible pricing, which means that depending on the season, you could earn more in a month than what you'd get from using the property as a long-term rental. It's also important to note that such statistical assessments don't cut across all neighborhoods, and there are many instances where the reverse might be true.

Therefore, to sum this up, research and understand the location before you make a choice, because in the rental business, location is one of the key determinants of profitability. People have failed in the past with some of the best investment strategies by simply choosing the wrong location for their investment. Don't fall into that trap!

Chapter 5: Start Your Airbnb Locally for a Quick Profit to Zoom Your Profits

There are many ways to invest in Airbnb. For a beginner, it's always safe to start from where you are, your neighborhood. Since you live there, you probably understand its dynamics better. Besides, you might not necessarily need to hire a real estate agent in your neighborhood because you can simply stroll around, and get to know the neighborhood. If need be, however, there's nothing wrong with working with a professional. Even in your neighborhood, you might still find their services quite useful.

As you grow in the business, you might see it fit to expand your operation to other neighborhoods. At this point, you'll be scaling up, so it will be best to work with professionals who understand those neighborhoods better. While some knowledge is transferable from one neighborhood to another, not all knowledge is. Even if you target the same audience, the market demographics will not be the same, neither will the available amenities, so when you start thinking of scaling up, get on the phone, and find yourself some professional realtors, property appraisers, inspectors, and any other contractor you'll need along the way.

So, let's get back to basics. You are setting up your first Airbnb in your neighborhood. How do you go about it?

First, you need to understand what's allowed on Airbnb, which pretty much is anything and everything, as long as it is habitable and meets the basic standards of living quarters as per the laws applicable in your location. To this end, Airbnb realized that there are so many kinds of living spaces that could be used as accommodation, and accepts three broad classifications:

- Shared room: Guests share the same living quarters with other guests, yourself, or your family.

- Private room: Guests will share some spaces or facilities with other guests, or even with yourself or your family. However, they are entitled to a private living area which they don't share with anyone.

- Entire place: In this case, you leave the entire property to your guests, giving them access to all facilities and amenities.

Other than the classifications above, Airbnb also recognizes the need or potential in sharing space and accepts other options like allowing guests to pitch a tent in your backyard, or providing an air mattress for additional guests. In line with the categories mentioned, you can list your property in anything from apartments to homes, tents, boats, RV, or even a castle, if you own one, your majesty!

Seeing that there are many options available, transparency is of utmost importance. When describing your property in your listing, be honest about what it is, and provide photos to prove it. At the end of the day, guests should get what they see online, and more importantly, should not have any problems or nasty surprises with your setup. To shed some light on this requirement, Airbnb expects that your listing meets the following conditions:

- The listing is solely used for lodging. Therefore, you cannot use your RV as an ice-cream truck during the day, and turn it into an Airbnb at night.

- Speaking of RVs, if you are hosting on a movable residence, like boats, yachts, and RVs, you must park in a privately owned area, or a semi-permanent location. This is important for security reasons. If your mobile residence does not meet these location requirements, it will not be allowed.

- Your listing must accurately represent the property on the ground, from the description to the exact location.

Not to burst your bubble, but if your property does not meet the minimum requirements above, there's a good chance it will pose a security risk, both to your guests and yourself, so you'll have to rethink that option. If your property qualifies, let's proceed and look at some regulations that will determine your profitability, and more importantly, whether you can even operate an Airbnb in your desired location in the first place.

How Do I Begin My Airbnb Journey?

The Law! That's the shortest answer to our question above.

Everything starts and ends with the law where business is concerned. You don't necessarily need a law degree to start an Airbnb, but you certainly need to understand the implications of certain laws in your jurisdiction.

The first thing you should understand is that your short-term rental company does not work for Airbnb and is not a subsidiary of Airbnb. Therefore, if you are ever in breach of any local laws, you will be on your own. There's only so much that Airbnb can do to protect you where local legislation is concerned, and in most cases, this can only apply where Airbnb bears liability. As a rule of thumb, therefore, Airbnb will not give you legal advice. They can only provide general guidelines where applicable, to help you understand your legal position according to their interpretation of your local laws that directly or explicitly apply to them. As far as your business is concerned, have a local attorney who understands the legislation on short-term rentals, and more importantly, legislation applicable to businesses that operate in the booming "sharing economy" like Airbnb and Uber.

That being said, here are some of the legal requirements that will generally apply to hosts in most places:

Building and Housing Standards

These standards generally stipulate the minimum acceptable design, construction, and maintenance standards for buildings. The objective here is to uphold certain standards of safety and health, ensuring that the residences are habitable. To this end, some local governments will schedule a property inspection to ensure you are hosting guests in spaces that are worthy of habitability.

Building Licenses

In most places, you must obtain a business license from your relevant local authorities to operate a short-term rental. This is a straightforward process, and you will find most or all the information you need by visiting the local government office or their website. Your attorney can also assist with this

Special Permits

In areas where the applicable laws are not quite clear on short-term rentals, your local authorities might come up with special permits for Airbnb hosts. Special permits give your business legality without being sucked into the legal conundrum presented by the absence of clearly defined laws on short-term rentals.

Other rules and permits that we can include in this category include HOAs, co-op rules, timeshare ownership and leases, because their rules and regulations vary in every neighborhood. In most cases, your landlord will be best-placed to advise you on what's applicable in your case if you decide to invest in a short-term rental on their property.

Tax Obligation

You have to pay your taxes. Today many local administrations collect tax from Airbnb hosts, so it's important to understand whether this applies to you, and how it works. Where Airbnb collects and remits tax on your behalf, they will inform you. On the other hand, in cases where you have to do it on your own, you might need a tax attorney to help you figure it out. You might also not be required to collect or remit any taxes, so seek clarity from your local authorities on this.

Tenancy Agreement

Your tenancy agreement could become the reason for your undoing, especially for guests who stay longer. In some places, tenants enjoy certain privileges once they stay on a property for a given duration of time. In such cases, once a guest exceeds the set threshold, they legally acquire tenancy rights. Under local tenancy laws, this might make it difficult for you to evict them without going through the predefined eviction proceedings as per the normal landlord–tenant agreement. This becomes a problem especially when your guests become a nuisance, either to you or your neighbors.

Zoning Laws

Even if you own the property, either by building or you bought it, zoning laws are instituted to create a sense of order in neighborhoods. Without them, people could modify their homes in a manner that makes them dangerous, invade the privacy of their neighbors, or any other reason that makes living around them a nuisance.

Zoning laws are outlined in city ordinances, planning codes, or zoning codes, and set out clear rules on what's considered acceptable usage of your home. It's always wise to consult your local authorities, and discuss your upcoming investment to ensure you are investing in a business model that adheres to the local zoning laws.

Local authorities were late to the party and ended up playing catch-up with legislation to impose some sanity in the industry in light of Airbnb's growth. That being said, there's been renewed calls all over the world to bring more oversight into the sector, especially when you consider the fact that local authorities are eyeing tax revenue from Airbnb hosts. With this in mind, you can expect more development in this sector over the years as Airbnb keeps working with authorities to come up with appropriate legislation for their business model.

Airbnb's promise, therefore, is to keep cooperating with local authorities in helping them realize their value proposition to local communities, especially in creating jobs and helping more people realize their dream of having a steady stream of passive income.

Ultimately, rules can be confusing, especially since there's no one-size-fits-all for Airbnb hosts. What is acceptable in your city might not be applicable in the city you wish to expand your operation into. Therefore, even as Airbnb collaborates with local authorities and governments all over the world to help create a clearer picture of the applicable laws, your best move, once again, is to consult a competent attorney.

Get Your Airbnb up and Running

The legal implications aside, let's now get you ready for your investment. At this point, your attorney has given you the green light, so it's full steam ahead. Contrary to what most people believe, getting started as an Airbnb host is actually quite easy. Here are five simple steps to help you set up and start welcoming guests:

Find an Ideal Space

One of the best things about the Airbnb platform is the unlimited options you have in terms of space you can rent out. As long as it meets Airbnb's standards on habitability, you are good to go.

Start anywhere, with whatever you can afford. It could be anything from a spare room in your apartment to your second home. Assuming that you don't own any of those, you can still invest in Airbnb as a co-host, or through rental arbitrage.

Furnish Your Airbnb

With the location under wraps, think of the kind of furnishing you need to make it stand out. The goal here is to create an amazing listing that gives your guests an amazing vacation experience. Start simple, and work your way up gradually.

For starters, don't complicate things. Use furnishings that give your space a touch of functionality. Keep your target audience in mind, because beginner-level furnishing for backpackers is not the same as what you'll do if you are targeting families.

Get Your Team Ready

As much as this is your baby, you'll need help from different people to get things moving. A solid team means getting your cleaners, handypersons, photographer, accountant, emergency contacts, and so on.

While you might be enthusiastic about doing it all on your own, it might not be the best strategy for you. The best way to succeed in this business is learning when to work with other people. Outsourcing is actually one of the smartest things you can do in this line of work.

Prepare Your Listing

As soon as you have everyone and everything ready, you can proceed to create the listing. Creating your listing basically means you are ready to host. When it comes to the listing, some of the things you should take into consideration include the title you'd want guests to identify your property with, the kind of guests you hope to host, your cleaning fees, marketing approach, whether you allow guests to book instantly, and more importantly, your cancellation policy.

These are crucial because they help you filter guests accordingly, so you don't end up with troublesome guests who cost you money and peace of mind. Before you publish your listing, have someone else look through it to give a second opinion. They might just catch something you didn't and help you with some honest feedback.

Once your listing is up, this isn't the end. If anything, your work has just begun. To ensure your property remains attractive to guests, you must continually commit to review and improve it. Read guest reviews, and see what you can change about the property. Talk to guests in person before they leave if you can, to get their opinion on how to make the property even better.

As far as marketing your property is concerned, consider anything and everything that you can use. Nothing is off limits. From search-engine optimization (SEO) to advertising your listing on social media, use everything in your arsenal.

One of the best ways to understand what your property offers guests is to spend some time in the property. Take a day or two, and live in your house like a guest. This gives you a real perspective of what your guests go through. You might even realize a thing or two that could be improved. For example, maybe the mattress is not as comfortable as you thought it was, or your internet connection might be unstable. Guests seek convenience, and if they can't find it in your home, it won't deliver that memorable experience, which eventually translates to losing customers.

Get Your Landlord on Board

Like most first-time Airbnb hosts, you probably don't own the property. You are working on a rental arbitrage model, where you have an arrangement with your landlord to use their property as a vacation rental. Note that this, for business purposes, might require a separate contract other than the tenancy agreement you signed to use the property as the tenant. Whether you are the original tenant and you wish to change your contract to a short-term rental, or if you want to run the business from the very beginning, you must sit down with your landlord, and discuss your options.

Let's look at the landlord's position for a moment, so you understand why this might not be as easy a conversation as you might hope it will be.

Your landlord is probably keeping this house for rental income. This, to them, is as much an investment into their future financial security as you hope it will be for you, if they allow you to run an Airbnb business. So, when you tell the landlord you wish to run a business, they imagine strange people coming and going from their property. They have probably read lots of horror stories about difficult guests and the kind of damage that they do to their property, so your landlord will naturally be apprehensive.

Put yourself in their shoes, you would too. Besides, to your landlord, you are a tenant. This means that if it ever serves your purpose, there's nothing stopping you from waking up one day and giving them a notice to terminate your tenancy contract. Your landlord is also looking at the potential complications arising with their insurance contract. For someone who hopes for a steady flow of rental income from this property, you see how this can become a problem for your landlord, right?

Now, the apprehension aside, your landlord doesn't have to reject your idea. All you have to do is talk to them, and try to persuade them to see things differently. You might make some promises, and you might have to sign a contract, so be careful not to promise more than you can deliver. Note that your landlord still has the right to evict you from the property if they ever feel the situation is untenable, or you cannot honor your agreement.

As a rule of thumb, do not go against your landlord's wishes. If your landlord rejects the idea, move along and look for another property. Your landlord might accept your suggestion, but the resident HOA might not. In this case, it will not work. By all means, do not try to run a secret Airbnb because you will be found out, and you stand to lose the most when this happens.

There's the irreparable damage in the relationship, trust, and mutual respect you've shared with your landlord at stake. In the worst possible case, your landlord might sue for breach of contract, leaving you facing eviction, the prospect of losing prepaid rent and security deposits, or liable for any damages that the law might see fit.

Before you talk to your landlord, take a moment, and consider the possible reasons why they might be apprehensive of the idea. Some landlords are naturally unreceptive to this idea, because they don't comprehend the dynamics of the sharing economy. The same applies to landlords who are not tech-savvy. Once you understand their perception, it might be easier for you to talk to them, or even accept their rejection.

Landlords might be difficult, but it's not impossible to persuade them. If you've been a tenant for a long time, you might leverage your relationship with them. Here are some possible strategies that might help you get some leeway with your landlord:

- Be honest about your intention to use this to supplement your income, which will also make it easier for you to keep paying rent, and increase the chances of extending your contract with them once the lease comes to term.

- Express your intention and commitment to maintain the property at the highest possible standards. Explain to your landlord that Airbnb has strict guidelines on cleanliness, maintenance, and order, and that you intend to uphold the same.

- Extend your gratitude by offering them a share of your earnings from the business over and above what you pay them as rent. You could also offer to finance any improvements and renovations that add value to their property. You'll have to discuss this with them, of course.

- On their insurance concerns, discuss the possibility of taking additional insurance cover to protect their investment beyond the cover they already have under their rental or landlord insurance policy. This might also be a good time to mention Airbnb's Host Guarantee and their cover against personal liability and property damage.

Since your landlord is primarily concerned about securing their investment, you can offer to take responsibility for some damages and include this in an amended contract. You could also top up the security deposit your landlord holds by virtue of your original contract with them.

What if I Don't Have Money?

Going by the discussions we've had in this book and what you'll come across everywhere else, it's easy to assume that Airbnb is only for those who have money. Not everyone enjoys the luxury of owning a home, or having some spare space in their house, or even getting a landlord that allows them to proceed with the idea. Naturally, the biggest challenge for most beginners in this industry is lack of capital, as is the case with many other industries. On the bright side, this should not stop you from realizing your dream.

Having a lot of money to start an Airbnb business is one of the biggest misconceptions you can ever buy into, and if you do, it will only block your thought process while other people start from scratch, and grow their businesses. While owning property guarantees you a bigger share of the profits, it is not the only way to invest in Airbnb, and you should not limit yourself to that notion. Here are some smart moves you can make on the platform without money:

Airbnb Experiences

You can also venture into the Airbnb business by selling experiences, for example, offering tour guide services. This is particularly a brilliant idea if you live in a location with lots of tourist attractions. Experiences are awesome for guests who need more than just a place to stay. This is where you come in, showing them around, especially those who don't want the cookie-cutter approach that tours and travel companies use. As their guide, your selling point is a personal touch. Tour companies mostly take guests to the same places where they probably have contractual arrangements with the establishments. You can, however, go the extra mile, and show customers even better experiences.

Property Management

Property managers are some of the most important people in this business. They come through for hosts who are too busy to manage their vacation rentals on their own. Of all the professionals that you will come across in this business, none earns as much as property managers do.

You'll also need to brush up on your property management skills, learn how to collaborate and supervise cleaners and other professionals in the industry. As a property manager, the property owner relies on your effort to ensure their property is well-maintained and keeps attracting guests, so your hard work will certainly pay off.

Local Rentals

As you stroll around the neighborhood, identify properties with open rental signs. Talk to their owners about turning them into short-term rentals on Airbnb. Of course, not all owners will be up for the idea, but some might. After all, it costs nothing to ask, and you might just stumble upon a life-changing opportunity.

Affiliate Marketing

Affiliate marketing is one of the oldest and biggest wealth-generating methods in the world. This is basically word-of-mouth marketing, using referrals from family, friends and acquaintances. Affiliates earn through commissions, so all you have to do is invite people to book the property and earn from their stay.

As you can see above, you are not limited by finances. Your dream to make it big on Airbnb can start from anywhere and as long as you have the passion and determination for it, you'll be well on your way to creating that steady flow of passive income that ushers you into a world of financial freedom in the future.

Chapter 6: Details to Guarantee My Successful Airbnb

What makes your listing pop on Airbnb?

From the moment you create your host account, this is one question that will always be on your mind. It's not just about making your listing pop, but also ensuring that it becomes a guest-favorite. Take a moment and look at some of the top properties by customer ratings on Airbnb, and you might notice some unique features that cut across most, if not all of them. While customer ratings might not tell you so much about the property, taking a glimpse at the property profiles could give you a hint of what you should strive to achieve for your listing.

In all fairness, people like different things, so even with your best effort, you might still not be able to please everyone. However, you don't need to please everyone. Instead, you need to create a listing with a natural charm that lures guests in at first glance. There are many things you can do to make your listing stand out from the crowd. As a long-term investment, you must also keep refreshing your listing from time to time to ensure it remains a guest-favorite. Since we cannot cover all the changes you can make to boost your profile, we'll focus on five key factors that will be crucial in elevating your profile and giving you the visibility you desire.

Invest in Quality Photos

Photography is a way of feeling, of touching, of loving. What you have caught on film is captured forever...it remembers little things, long after you have forgotten everything.–Aaron Siskind

Your listing is one of the greatest projects you'll ever create, so you must be proud of it. You've put in so much effort for guests to feel at home and enjoy it. In a platform that's flooded with properties, there's no better way to appeal to potential guests than to show them what your property is all about. This is where professional photography comes in.

Of course, you're probably thinking *why not just take some nice photos with your phone and upload them, right?* Well, while your phone can take some amazing photos, you might not be able to get that professional touch that sells. Online audiences today have a very short attention span, which means that you have an increasingly diminishing window of opportunity to get people's attention. This is why you need professional photos for your listing. With professionally done shots, you have a higher chance of getting more profile views and attracting more guests while you're at it. You'll probably also have more users saving or bookmarking your property for future reference, or even better, sending you a message to find out more about your booking schedule.

Professional photography is an investment into your future, just in the same way your property is. Think about it for a moment. If you took photos with your phone, you'll probably want to take better photos when you upgrade to a better phone, and so on. On the other hand, professionally done photos can stay on your profile for years while you channel your energy to marketing your profile beyond Airbnb. This also creates a sense of consistency, which for your guests is a sign of trust.

For brand consistency, you'll market your listing with the same photos on Airbnb, Instagram, Booking.com, and any other platform. This also makes it easier for guests to recognize your listing wherever they come across it online, increasing your chances of getting repeat customers.

Despite your iPhone having some amazing features, professional photography gets you more benefits that will help you position your property as a winner, for example professional editing, special lenses, lighting 3D and drone shots, virtual staging, and the ability to accentuate rooms, layouts, and other aspects of your property.

Even better, professional photographers with experience in the real estate industry know what it takes to attract customers to your listing, making it easier to deliver a careful blend of shots that get the attention you desire from potential guests without compromising on your style.

While professional photos will be good for your profile, there's only so much that they can do for your property on their own. Photos go hand in hand with an elaborate description. Talk about your listing in a manner that tells the reader all they need to know about it. Remember that this is someone who has probably seen your photos already, so your description should be succinct, and help your guests feel like they have already checked into your property.

A compelling description makes your property more attractive to guests. Remember that these are people going away on a vacation, and however long or short it might be, they are looking for a memorable and pleasant experience. To this end, ensure your description and listing details are updated and relevant to the photos you've published online. If there are any unique features that might add more value to the listing, for example, that amazing cafe on the ground floor, or the fact that guests will enjoy beachfront access, be sure to highlight this in the description, including clear photos.

Furnishing Your Airbnb

Building on professional photos, your next step is tasteful furnishings. Your approach to furnishing your Airbnb will go a long way in boosting its appeal to guests because this is where you showcase your taste and style. You might not realize this yet, but furnishing plays an important role in setting the perfect experience guests seek when booking your property. This might also help you earn those five-star ratings.

Furnishing your property isn't just as simple as getting some furniture and calling it a day. You must put some thought into it. For instance, what kind of aesthetic are you going for? Are you looking for a contemporary feel or a rustic appeal? This sets the tone for everything else you'll do going forward and will also play into your marketing strategy.

Having decided on the look you are going for; you'll create a list of all the furnishings you need. Make this list as exhaustive as possible because you'll use it for future reference. Granted, you might not be able to buy everything you need right away but keeping them on a checklist will help you upgrade the property over time. The best approach for this is to create a list for each room. This makes your work easier with upgrades, improvements, and even checking the property for damages at the end of your guest's stay.

Fully aware of what you need for each room, your next step is drawing up a budget. A reasonable budget will help you furnish your property as you desire gradually so that you don't put pressure on finances. Remember that for your first property, or any other property for that matter, there's no guarantee that you'll have a consistent flow of guest traffic. Therefore, there might be times when you dig into your savings to keep the property running by paying for utility bills, repairs, and maintenance services.

By all means, your savings account should not pay for furnishings. You should have a budgetary allocation for property furnishings. Just like your personal household budget, you'll have to assess your list above, and identify needs from wants. Needs are those furnishings that are necessary for your rental to offer the basic services every guest expects. You cannot compromise on those ones. Wants are those furnishings that add a touch of oomph to your listing. You can do without them, but they might get you more attention. You must strike a delicate balance between the two so that you don't lose out on bookings because your property offers the bare minimum.

For your first investment, the secret is usually to combine a minimalist approach with tasteful or artistic placements. You can also leverage the natural lighting in the house to further accentuate the look and feel you seek. Here are some simple furnishing tips for different rooms that can help you create a winning listing.

The Bedroom

- Get a strong and stable bed that will guarantee you years of use.

- Avoid beds with removable legs. Generally, the fewer movable parts on the bed, the better.

- The extra space in storage beds can be useful for keeping spare linen and towels.

- Shop for good quality, comfortable mattresses.

- Invest in quality mattress covers.

- Memory foam mattresses are generally more affordable and easier to replace than spring mattresses.

- White beddings give your rooms a professional feel. Besides, white also tends to make rooms look bigger than they actually are.

- Guests will always appreciate a full-length mirror.

The Living Room

- Leather (real or faux) is too expensive to maintain, so avoid it altogether.

- The living room gets the most guest traffic, so prioritize functionality and durability for everything from furniture to carpets and rugs.

- Removable, washable covers will be a great investment.

- For dining and kitchen furniture and equipment, shop for items that can withstand wear and tear.

- As much as you emphasize functionality and durability, do not skimp out on comfort either.

The Bathroom

- For the bathroom, keep things simple but functional.

- If you provide hand or bath towels, always choose white as it's easier to spot dirt, clean, and maintain.

- Buy from the same places hotels and other players in the hospitality industry get their supplies, as these are generally built to withstand multiple use.

- Other basic amenities you should include in the bathroom are conditioner, shampoo, and anything else you would normally use in your house. Remember that when a guest checks in, they need to feel at home for their stay to be memorable.

The Kitchen

- For the kitchen, shop for durability and functionality over aesthetics.

- Most guests won't give your utensils the same care and attention you would, so it's best not to take chances on expensive and fragile items.

- Shop according to the needs of your target audience. If you allow parties in your property, it's wise to stock up on disposable plates and cutlery.

Finally, ensure you have a small trash can in each room. This can make your cleaners' work easier once your guests check out. For electronics and appliances, print out a small, laminated manual with instructions to guide your guests, lest they try to figure it out on their own and end up damaging the gadgets.

Pricing Strategy

Everything you've done so far to make your property more visible online plays into your profitability objective. At the end of the day, this is a business, and it is only fair that you get a decent return on your investment. Professional photos and tasteful furnishings can only get you so far. Next, you take things a notch higher, and implement a reasonable pricing strategy.

Naturally, you'll come across lots of properties that are furnished even better than yours but struggle to get bookings. This is because many beginner hosts don't understand how to implement dynamic pricing. You might inadvertently price yourself out of the market if you don't know how to set the ideal property prices. Let's look at some crucial factors that can help you adjust your rental prices for utmost profitability.

Key Performance Indicators (KPI)

Key performance indicators are measurable values that help you determine whether your business strategy is effective, and ultimately tell you whether you are running a profitable business or not. Common values for your Airbnb include the average daily rate, occupancy rate, operating expenses, and average duration guests stay in your property.

With this information, you can compare your total operating expenses against your income to determine the appropriate price range that keeps you in the game, even when your property is vacant. Such a price range also gives you a buffer so you never have to dig into your emergency savings account to sort out emerging issues in the rental.

Competitor Analysis

It's always good to know what other hosts are charging for similar properties, not just on Airbnb, but also on other platforms like Booking.com and VRBO. In your analysis, compare properties with similar amenities or those with better features that are priced in the same range as yours. Compare prices during peak and off-peak seasons, the holidays, and weekends, and try to understand the pricing trends and patterns throughout the year.

Identify a few properties and monitor their price changes. In your analysis, you should also remember that many hosts list new properties at discounted rates, usually up to 30% to attract guests and get reviews faster, eventually giving their new listings a popularity boost.

Your Bare Minimums

One of the harsh realities of short-term rentals that no one tells you about is that there comes a time when you work with the bare minimums. As much as everyone keeps talking about the insane amounts of money they make from Airbnb, the truth is that there are periods during the year when hosts operate on break-even rates. It's important, therefore, that you figure out the lowest possible rate you can offer, then work your way from there.

You arrive at the lowest possible rate by factoring in all your expenses including mortgage payments, utilities and other operating expenses. These estimates tell you the least amount you should earn per night to run a profitable vacation rental. With this information, you can comfortably offer discounts to attract guests to your listing.

Smart Pricing

One thing you'll appreciate about Airbnb is that they constantly come up with innovative ways to help hosts get the most out of their platform. Smart pricing is one of such approaches, which helps you capitalize on seasonal demand by varying your listing prices accordingly. This way, you can adjust your prices upwards when demand is high, for example, when there's an influx of visitors attending a special event in your city.

Seamless Check Ins and Outs

Every guest hopes that they won't have any trouble getting in or out of your property. This is actually the first point of contact your guest has with you away from the app, so it's important to make it as convenient as possible. Provide all the necessary information so the check-in process can be as smooth as possible. First impressions do matter, and even if your property is remotely managed, this is the first point where you earn or lose the guest's confidence.

How easy is it to get to your property? This is something many people take lightly, yet it matters a lot to guests. Whether your property is in a rural location or not, ease of access is of utmost importance to your guests. Share an updated and accurate map of the neighborhood. Your guest might also appreciate parking information, for example, reserved parking, no parking areas, or a parking pass if available.

Once a booking is confirmed, share any information that might be relevant to your guest. A check-in guide can also be useful, just in case you have additional instructions that might help your guest have an enjoyable experience. For example, we had earlier talked about special instructions or manuals for electronics and gadgets in your house. Leave your guest a simple note about this. This is important because one of the first things many guests do as soon as they check into your house is to turn on the TV, home theater system, or any other entertainment system. Leave a note about the Wi-Fi password, door code, and any other thing your guest might need. More importantly, encourage your guest to ask about anything that they might not be sure about.

Another useful idea is to share emergency contact information, so your guest knows who to call if things get out of hand, especially if you are not the emergency contact. At times it's better to try and solve some problems instead of letting them escalate and involve local authorities.

Finally, your guest's stay is almost coming to an end. Just like the check-in process, checking out should also be a walk in the park. Unnecessarily complex check-out processes can be frustrating, especially when your guest is on a deadline, for example, rushing to catch a flight. Don't wait for the last minute to get things going. Send your guest instructions in good time, so they know where to leave your keys and any other instructions you might feel necessary to share with them before they leave.

For planning purposes, you can send check-out instructions a day before, so your guest has enough time to get things in order. Don't be too pushy in your message or appear to be kicking them out. Remember that your guest is still on vacation in your property, so they don't want to feel rushed out of your property.

As the end of their stay approaches, many guests tend to mentally focus on the next step in their trip, probably their next destination. Therefore, this might not be the best time to ask for reviews or feedback. Ideally, you can send a follow-up message the next day, thanking them for choosing your property for their holiday, and softly nudging them to review your listing and recommend it to their acquaintances.

The Power of Automation

Automation is one of the smartest strategies you can implement in your Airbnb. It will make your work easier, and give your guests autonomy while in your house. This way, you can both get on with your days without interference. When implemented properly, automation helps you eliminate time and resource wastage by scheduling recurring tasks where necessary. Common tasks that can be automated include writing guest reviews, managing your booking calendar, adjusting your nightly pricing to seasonal demand, or managing cleaning activities after your guest checks out.

We spend or waste a lot of time attending to mundane and repetitive tasks like the ones mentioned above, time that could be well-spent on other productive things. Automation essentially improves your productivity, and with more time and resources at your disposal, you can look into ways of growing your business. Let's look at some common areas where you can implement automation in your property for greater returns below:

Property Management

The whole point of automation is to limit the time you spend on mundane tasks. As far as managing your rental is concerned, there are a number of tasks that you can move off your schedule by automation. These include creating and tracking tasks for your cleaners, handypersons, and any other contractor, managing bookings, and automated communication with your guests.

As your business grows, you might not be able to handle all these tasks on your own. Therefore, it would make sense to bring in professionals. Guests check in and leave your properties at different times, so it's also not easy to have a regular cleaning schedule. With the right property management platform, all you have to do is schedule cleaning services as soon as a guest checks out, and your cleaners will be informed they have some work to do.

Smart Utilities and Gadgets

One area where automation will come in handy is in the use of smart devices in your property. We are in the age of the Internet of Things (IoT), and there are lots of electronic devices in the house that you can automate. For utmost comfort, your guests can simply set their desired temperature inside the house if you have a smart thermostat.

Sensors fitted into the IoT devices help with automation, making it easier for you to access them as long as they are connected to your internet network. This can actually be a good security feature in some cases. For example, you could remotely turn on the lights and music in your property, giving the impression that someone's home, even though the property is vacant. Such features can protect your property from petty theft.

Cleaning and Maintenance

There's a good chance that you won't be handling the property cleaning on your own, and even if that were the case, you'll have to clean the property as soon as a guest checks out, because someone else might book the property right away.

If you are like most hosts and you outsource cleaning services, all you have to do is make arrangements with your cleaners, so they know what to do. Once that is done, they'll step in as soon as your guest is off the premises and do their job. This saves you a lot of time. Besides, you don't have to keep calling your cleaners to find out whether they are available to do the job. The beauty of this is that your property will always be clean and ready for guests, even if you are unavailable or unreachable.

While automation is a brilliant idea, you'll still need to check in on things from time to time, mostly to ensure that all your integrated systems are working as they should. The oversight role is just as important to your overall success as the automation processes, because without it, you could easily end up automating failure in processes and procedures that work against you.

At this point, you can now go back, and review the top properties we mentioned at the beginning of this chapter. You'll realize that the factors we've discussed above apply to most of them. That should tell you something about how to position your property for greatness. One of the best things about Airbnb is that you can always learn from what other hosts are doing, not necessarily by meeting the hosts or visiting their properties in person, but by simply checking out their listings and reading the guest reviews on their profiles. If you do this, you'll certainly pick up some useful ideas on how to make your property pop, and even stay ahead of your competitors by introducing unique features that might be a hit in other areas but are yet to be introduced in your location. As far as improving your property is concerned, the only thing at the back of your mind should be *renew, refresh, and refine*!

Chapter 7: The Ten Commandments of a Successful Airbnb

It's beyond doubt that Airbnb is an incredible investment opportunity. As a host, there's so much potential in this business that can bring you closer to achieving your financial goals. That being said, you cannot also ignore the fact that this will not be a walk in the park. Setting up an Airbnb isn't just about getting a house, furnishing it, and posting it online. The biggest challenge is honoring your commitment to the process. Your success in this business is an all-encompassing process that includes guest management, customer relations, marketing, prudent financial and accounting skills, and property management. You must, therefore, invest as much of your time as you'll invest your money to have a shot at success. More importantly, this is also a learning opportunity, and the more you educate yourself about customer needs, applicable legislation, taxation, and other aspects of the industry, the better an investor you'll become.

To survive in this industry, you'll need someone to hold your hand from time to time. Competition is stiff, and there will be moments when you might even consider quitting altogether. Like other businesses, your resilience will go a long way. Embrace new knowledge, network, and try to grow your relationships with other hosts. You will learn a lot about the industry and smart hacks that experienced hosts have used to prop their businesses especially during the lean months. To this end, arise, come ye forth, and learn the 10 commandments of running a successful Airbnb business.

Thou Shalt Ask For Feedback

Feedback goes a long way in this business. Hosts rely on guest reviews to boost rankings, while guests need good reviews and ratings from hosts to prove that they are decent people who deserve the good vacation ambience in your property. Suffice to say, reviews mean more to hosts than guests. Even if you reject a guest because you feel they might not meet your standards, another host might be desperate enough to take a chance on them. You, on the other hand, might be missing out on bookings and even have to lower your listing prices by virtue of low ratings.

Here's an interesting thing about reviews: go ahead and ask for them. There's no shame in asking, right? As long as you are asking politely and within a good timeframe, you'll get the ratings you seek. Guests don't just sit around and wait to write reviews. Some of them have busy schedules and might not remember to rate their stay. While Airbnb might send them a message to rate their experience, people generally ignore corporate emails. This is why you should send that email. There's a better chance they'll respond to your message, even though they ignored the same message from Airbnb. It gets even easier for you if the guest had a pleasant time on your property.

Even as you ask and wait for the review, keep an open mind because there's always a chance you might get a negative review. Some guests don't understand the ratings system and might give you a one-star rating thinking that they are rating you as number one. Others write bad reviews because of simple misunderstandings. Either way, don't let it get to your head. You can't always please everyone anyway, right? As long as you are doing the right thing by your convictions, getting more good reviews is all that matters.

Thou Shalt Become a Business-Minded Host

Airbnb can be the key that unlocks different levels of success for you. From growing your business to exploring your passions, each guest interaction is an opportunity to do something different, something better. You are now an entrepreneur, which means you must learn to think like one. Everything from understanding the market to guest interactions and managing your team of cleaners, handypersons, and other professionals who help you make your property an amazing vacation rental demands an entrepreneurial mindset.

What is your goal, vision, or mission for this business? Airbnb's mission, for example, is to encourage guests and hosts to understand that anyone can belong anywhere. This is the core philosophy that everyone working at the company's various offices buys into. This is the philosophy that guides and inspires all their actions and decisions. So, what about you? What drives you?

Why do you want to do this? Of course, there's the pursuit of financial freedom. However, the answer you seek is bigger than financial freedom. Just as Airbnb is the key to unlocking the doors to financial freedom, the answers you seek lie in the "what next?" once you achieve financial freedom. This is what drives you. This is what gives you purpose and the strength to keep going when the market is in a slump.

Business-minded hosts generally embrace a growth mindset. You see opportunities where most people see obstacles and difficulty. You see failure as a new beginning, a lesson that equips you with the skills to do, and become, better while others see failure as a dead end. You are positive in your approach, embrace challenges, and trust that your efforts are channeled towards the right cause. You are open to new ideas, are determined, and are not one to shy away from experimenting.

As a business-minded host, you are innovative, and endeavor to deliver nothing short of an amazing, memorable stay for your guests. This, with a bit of flexibility, will help you achieve more than success on Airbnb, it will also help you create and maintain quality connections in the industry with like-minded individuals from all over the world.

Thou Shalt Respect Your Guests

This is as simple as it gets, yet somehow, many hosts get this wrong. The whole point of running an Airbnb is to welcome guests and hope that they have a memorable stay in your property. If that's not happening, you are going about it the wrong way. While hosts generally record the most complaints about difficult customers, guests have equally laid bare their frustrations with some hosts. Respect is a two-way street, and it's only fair that you respect your guests throughout their stay in your property.

At the end of the day, you are hoping to get good reviews from your guests. Think of reviews like word-of-mouth marketing. While you'll put up a good description for your property, complete with professional photos, what sets your property from other tastefully furnished listings is the guest reviews.

Potential customers, especially those who have time, will read reviews to get a guest's opinion of your property and your demeanor if you are available. No one likes to go on a vacation and have their host poking their nose in their affairs all the time. There's a reason why it's called a getaway, right? You leave your pesky supervisors and bosses behind, and have some peace and quiet to yourself, or whatever else makes you feel relaxed and happy.

Respect means not invading your guest's space. Provide all the necessary information ahead of their check in so they have enough time to go over it. This way, your guest can ask you about anything they are not sure about. The approach here is to let the communication come from the guest, not the other way around.

While you don't have to be there in person, remind your guest that you'll be available to them if they ever need anything, and make good on that promise. You know the neighborhood better than your guest, so if they need it, you can share suggestions and recommendations on some exciting things they can do during their stay.

Remember Your Call of Duty and Keep it Sacred

In this business, it's so easy to get carried away in the pursuit of a steady stream of passive income that you forget the most important thing—to provide a memorable vacation experience for guests. Let's go back to basics for a moment. Airbnb is driven by the mission to belong anywhere, and this is what every host must abide by.

Granted, you are in this to make a profit and probably build your empire, but once you lose sight of the vision, greed sets in and you'll soon end up as one of those money-hungry hosts that people keep complaining about on social media.

If you are keen on discussions around Airbnb, you might have noticed that many people are of the opinion that hosts are getting greedier by the day, pushing guests back to hotels. If you remember correctly, Airbnb spearheaded the revolution that had hotels running scared, forcing most of them to rethink their business models and realign their strategies.

Indeed, there will be some difficult hosts from time to time, you just don't have to be one of them. As much as this is your property, your duty is to your guests, and driven by Airbnb's mission to belong anywhere, this is your calling. What this means is that despite a few difficult guests from time to time, you will strive to give your customers the royal treatment. Where possible, go over and above what you advertise in your listing to ensure your guests feel they are getting more value for their money. As a rule of thumb in this line of business, always overdeliver; never underdeliver.

Honor Thy Local Laws

Forget about the popular cliche that laws are meant to be broken. Laws establish order, and without order, all you have is chaos. Now imagine running your Airbnb in an environment overrun by chaos. You can be certain of one thing, that you won't make any money. This is why it's important to understand and follow the rules, from Airbnb's terms of engagement to the local laws as per your HOA, or local administration.

Laws don't just apply to you; they also apply to your guests by virtue of their presence in your property. It's important, therefore, that you do your best to ensure your guests understand this. This particularly applies to rules instituted by your landlord or the resident HOA. Guests who breach such rules can easily get you evicted from the neighborhood, giving up the benefit of the time and other resources you invested in this project.

Some of the common rules that you must communicate clearly to your guest include parking arrangements, instructions on hosting parties, and noise or loud music. These are things we tend to take for granted, but they can become quite an inconvenience when you contravene the instructions.

As far as laws are concerned, knowledge and preparation are the most important things. You must have everything ready before you invest in a certain neighborhood. Understand the local requirements and regulations because they will play a significant role in your profitability. Some cities have specific rules for home-sharing which might apply to tax requirements, licensing, the use of some buildings or zoning regulations that affect your business. Other than signing up on Airbnb, you might be required to obtain a license, permit, or be duly registered with the local authorities to start hosting. In some cases, you might also bear the responsibility of collecting and remitting taxes.

Thou Shalt Make a Good First Impression

The first few minutes of welcoming guests to your property can make or break your experience. Guests have high expectations when they book your property, so the challenge is on you to meet these expectations. First impressions last forever. One of the things people remember vividly about their holidays, vacations, and trips is that warm welcome.

Humans generally appreciate simple things. It only takes a few seconds for someone to decide whether they love your property or not. Given that their only experience with your property has been your online listing, guests make snap judgments once they see the property in person. Unfortunately, if the decision goes against you, you'll have an uphill task trying to change your guest's mind. This also explains why some guests book for a week or two, but check out after a day or two, seeking something better. At this point, your guest's mind is made up that they won't get value for their money from your property.

So, how can you avoid this?

Well, first impressions are everything. You don't even have to do something extravagant. At the end of the day, the whole point of a first impression is to impress your guest. Create that warm lasting memory that puts a smile on their face. Make it interesting, but professional. It doesn't even have to be personal, something as simple as a fast response time speaks volumes to your guests.

Once the booking is done, prepare a nice, warm welcome message or email. To make your work easier, create an email template so all you have to do is edit it with the new guest's information and send. In case you are present, you could easily pull off a lasting impression on your guest. Help them with the bags when they arrive. Welcome your guests home to the aroma of a pleasant snack, or a favorite from the local restaurant. Show them around the house or anything else you can do to make them feel welcome. Since people have different needs, tastes, and preferences, an in-person first impression might not be one of the easiest things to achieve, but if you do it right, it will pay off handsomely.

Thou Shalt Tap Into the Power of Outsourcing

You've read blogs about successful Airbnb hosts, watched some of their videos on YouTube, or even attended some webinars. These are the kind of grass to grace stories that uplift and encourage beginners to try their luck in the industry. Airbnb is largely a rewarding business model, with something for both hosts and guests. What you might not realize yet, however, is that you probably won't be able to do it all alone, hence the need for outsourcing.

There's nothing wrong with paying someone to do some of the mundane tasks for you. You must, however, research well and ensure you are outsourcing to the right person, or company. This isn't just another short-term rental business, this is your investment into your financial future. It makes sense, therefore, to ensure you are outsourcing to professionals who share the same vision of excellence and are committed to delivering the best services.

Compare different service providers first, and more importantly, the cost of their services. This will eat into your income, so you have to ensure you are getting the best value for your money. Ultimately, you are not just outsourcing some tasks, you are getting a business partner. Outsourcing will save you time and money, and if it's done right, could increase your revenues. Think about it for a moment, the people who clean your property have friends and family members who might be looking for a nice Airbnb for a few days. They could certainly send some referrals your way.

Another instance where outsourcing could be useful is in handling your accounting and revenue management. At the end of the day, you are running a business, so you'll have to pay taxes and pay for other stuff too. You could outsource these tasks to a competent bookkeeper. Focus on what you are good at, perhaps marketing your listing online, and so on, and tap into someone else's professional profile for other aspects of your business.

Thou Shalt Never Keep Your Guests Waiting

Guests are everything. Without them, hosts would have no one to attend to. Even in normal life situations, imagine yourself as a guest, showing up to an event or an agreed meeting point on time, only for your host to keep you waiting. It's one of those frustrating situations that proves that your host lacks personal etiquette, or even worse, has no respect for your time.

Fast-forward to an online hosting experience where you have paid your hard-earned money to spend a few days in someone's house, yet for some reason, they keep you waiting. This, honestly, isn't the best way to start a vacation. In most cases, things only go south from here. As a rule of thumb, always have everything ready for your guest as soon as possible. Plan in advance so you can avoid the last-minute rush.

Interestingly enough, your response time could also land you in trouble with guests, especially those who make last-minute bookings. People have different reasons for waiting until the last moment to book their stay, and unfortunately, you can't fault them for that. You can't also predict how events will unfold in your day, so at times your inability to respond on time might be unavoidable. You can, however, make arrangements to prevent this by automating your customer interactions, or outsourcing communication to professionals. This way, your guests will always have someone attending to them even if you are having one of those chaotic days.

As it turns out, response time is one of the key factors that Airbnb algorithms take into consideration when showing listings. Hosts who respond faster generally enjoy more favor in the search results than those who take longer to respond to guests. Response rate is one of the factors that count toward you being assigned a Superhost status on Airbnb, so if you look at the bigger picture, this commandment is meant to help you.

Thou Shalt Not Post an Incomplete Listing

There's nothing as bad as an incomplete listing because all it does is show potential guests that you don't care. If you are not bothered to provide a complete listing, what's to say you'll be bothered to ensure the residence will be worth the memorable experience your guest is hoping for?

Once you decide to run an Airbnb, the first step is listing your property. If you get this wrong, everything else will probably not go well for you. One important aspect of listing your property is to ensure you have a description good enough to welcome guests. Whether you are listing the entire property or shared space, you must bring a professional touch to it. The way you handle the listing will determine how successful your property will be online. Think of your listing as your trusted sales agent. If they are not competent, you won't make any sales.

A professional approach to your listing is important because this is where you describe your property so that when someone goes through the listing, they are convinced that this is the perfect spot for their vacation. Some useful information that should never be missing from your listing includes your house rules and any special facilities or amenities available, like wheelchair access. Not all properties have special facilities like wheelchair access and guests don't always look for it, but if you have it, list it. You could also indicate that your property is run fully on solar, if that's true. It might not seem relevant at the time, but rest assured this is one of those things that could earn you more guests, especially the curious kind and the environmentally conscious ones.

Finally, and this is so important, make sure you don't lie in your listing. Misleading guests hardly ever works because they'll still write a review at the end of their stay, and lying won't look good on your profile. As much as you are trying to beat the competition, be genuine and honest about what you have and what you don't have. Honesty, as they say, is often the best policy.

Thou Shalt Not Disrespect Airbnb

Respect goes a long way in this and any other business. To succeed in this life, you must learn to respect people, property, and rules. In the Airbnb business, mutual respect between guests and hosts helps to create an amazing environment where everyone thrives and is happy with their experience. It's safe to say that mutual respect is the glue that binds hosts, guests, and the entire Airbnb ecosystem together, forging towards the vision to belong anywhere.

Unfortunately, not everyone subscribes to the gospel of mutual respect. People come from different backgrounds and some people simply are of questionable character. To this end, Airbnb put in place a number of measures to level the playing field so that every participant in their ecosystem can get value from their product. For hosts, you hope to get decent guests who will treat your property with dignity, enjoy a good stay, and hopefully come back or send you referrals. For guests, they hope to find an amazing residence that guarantees them that memorable vacation they badly need, and if all goes well, bookmark it for future reference.

So, where does the disrespect come in? Well, everything seems good until one of you suggests payment off the Airbnb platform. As people usually like to say, cutting out the middleman, which in this case, is Airbnb. There's nothing wrong with trying to save some money on a transaction, but you should also understand that there's a reason why Airbnb puts such measures in place. First, keeping all communication and transactions on the Airbnb platform makes it easier for Airbnb to assist you in the event of a dispute because they have all evidence of your interaction with guests. If you go against this and something goes awry with your guest, you are on your own. Besides, you'll have no proof that this person was ever a guest on your property, or that they failed to pay as agreed.

On a personal note, you must think of your property not like any other business, but as an investment into your future. All the rules and regulations put in place by Airbnb are to safeguard your investment. This is also why you are protected under their Host Guarantee program. Therefore, be smart, and choose the safest option. Stay on the platform.

Chapter 8: Don't Just Think About It...DO IT!

We've had quite a journey, all the way from discussing the history of Airbnb, the belong anywhere ideology, to the ten most important things that can help you succeed in the industry. This knowledge can only be useful if you put it to good use, and that's the point of this final chapter. Whether you are reading this book from your tablet, listening to an audio copy or any other file format you prefer, you have to ask yourself, *what's next?* Where do you go from here? How do you turn this information into actionable steps?

From all the success stories you might have come across online, it's clear that Airbnb is a timely resource. Whether you are looking for a side hustle, a new investment in your portfolio, or any other reason, Airbnb can be a reliable source of passive income. If you've been wondering how you can set yourself up for financial freedom in the future, this is how you make your first move. In the sections below, we'll share some insight on useful strategies that will help you set foot in the right direction, start the right way, and grow a successful Airbnb business

How to Get More Airbnbs Going

Let's face it, if you are going to succeed on Airbnb, one listing probably won't be enough. Success in this case, means running a business that nets you a six-figure income, or even higher. To achieve this goal, your efforts must be centered around growth from the very beginning. Just so we are clear, you are tapping into Airbnb's massive potential to create a steady stream of income, passive or otherwise, that will usher you into the much-coveted dream of financial freedom.

So, how do you go from your first listing to owning a portfolio of Airbnb listings? Well, the secret is to capitalize on the listing you already have. Here are some simple tips to help you:

Honesty Is the Best Policy

One of the best things a guest can say about your property is that it was as advertised. This means using photos and the listing description to create a vivid picture in the guest's mind of what they can expect. The short-term rental business is a relationship business, so you must make a good first impression. If anything, you only have one chance to impress potential guests, and they'll definitely talk about it in your reviews.

From time to time, guests are disappointed when they check into a listing and realize it's a far cry from what they saw online. Nothing ruins your reputation faster than disgruntled guests, so don't oversell your property beyond what it truly is.

Prompt Communication

Everyone appreciates honest, clear, and proactive communication. You must stay in touch with your guests from the moment they book to the time they check out of your property. As soon as your guests book your property, you can find out useful information like special arrangements for children, dietary requirements, allergies, pet needs, and so on.

While most guests won't need more than the basic services and facilities available, taking a keen interest in the finer details will go a long way in ensuring your guests have a memorable experience. Besides, asking this information beforehand gives you ample time to prepare. Your guests will certainly appreciate the fact that you took a keen interest in their welfare.

On your side, the nature of communication gives you an idea of the kind of guests you'll be hosting.

Dedication to Your Guests

This can be a tricky one, but in most cases, it works out well for hosts. Try and check in on your guests after the first night to find out if everything is okay, or if they had any challenges settling in. It is a tricky one because some guests simply want to be left alone and feel that if they needed anything, they would reach out to you.

However, it is generally a good idea to check up on your guests. For someone whose only encounter with your property has so far been the description and listing photos on Airbnb, this can be a good opportunity to get their opinion, perhaps some complaints, or suggestions on what they feel you could do better to make their stay memorable.

Instead of waiting until the end of their stay for a review, you get an early chance to impress your guests, which will work to your advantage in the long run. Remember that your ultimate goal is to keep your guests happy, especially since your entire growth plan rests on the success of your first listing.

Guest Appreciation

Your guests could have chosen any other property on Airbnb but checked into yours. For that, you should be grateful. It doesn't hurt to say a little thank you to your guest for choosing your listing. Assuming you haven't had any complaints or concerns so far, send that thank you note at the end of their stay. Remind your guest how important they are to your business, and politely ask for a positive review. This increases the chances of your guest writing a positive review about your listing, especially if they did have a good time on your property.

While Airbnb will nudge guests to write reviews after their stay, some guests tend to ignore these messages altogether while some innocently forget. There's no shame in asking your guest to write a review. You could send that reminder as soon as they check out, a day or week later, whichever works for you.

Are Some Locations Better Than Others?

In the real estate business, some properties will always be better than others. There are many reasons for this, from location to the owner's choice of furnishing. It makes sense, therefore, that the same concept applies to short-term rentals. Properties of the same size and facilities will attract different rates on Airbnb. To understand why this happens, we must look at the key factors that make a property ideal for investment.

Using this approach, it will also be easier to learn how to identify ideal or promising locations for your investment. As has been mentioned adversely in this book, location will always be one of the most important factors that influence your profitability and potential for success in this business. Let's have a look at some of these unique factors that will be useful when comparing different property locations below:

Low Competition

Competition is great for the growth of any industry. It forces business owners to think outside the box, innovate, and improve their business models. In the vacation rentals business, the same applies, but to some extent, when you are comparing profitability for two locations, competition favors guests more than hosts.

For guests, a highly competitive market means that hosts will constantly try to outdo one another. Such a market will have a lot of offers, discounts, and promotions. Hosts will also offer more facilities and amenities at a considerably low price. For hosts, this cut-throat system is too strenuous and might not be worth it in the long run, especially if you consider the overall costs of running your property.

A good location for a host, therefore, is one with low competition. Low competition means that there are fewer hosts in the area for the average number of guests who seek accommodation. Granted, the absence of competition might stifle creativity because hosts are under no pressure to innovate. However, a location with low competition from short-term rentals and hotels is good for you, especially if the occupancy rates are considerably higher. In such locations, you can comfortably charge higher than other areas. As the competition increases, you might have to consider charging lower to keep your property occupied most of the year.

Laws and Regulations

The law has recently caught up with Airbnb, hosts, and guests alike, and in jurisdictions where the confines of the law are not quite clear, the outcome can be messy. As an investor, it's important to put your money in an area with clear laws, especially if the laws are lenient or favorable. This is the challenge that faces Airbnb hosts today.

You could research and find a decent location with good demand for vacation rentals, but all this could be worthless if the local laws don't create an enabling business environment. With more local authorities engaging Airbnb on the best way to apply taxes and other legal requirements, it's even more important for you to understand how this affects your profitability in the long run.

In some areas, the laws are so strict that it becomes pointless to invest altogether. It's so bad that Airbnbs are illegal in some places. In such areas, there's no point in investing because you will risk it all for nothing. You might end up facing hefty fines or worse.

You will also come across some areas where even though running an Airbnb business is completely legal, there are some restrictions attached that impede your profitability. To estimate your potential earnings, you must consider fees and taxes payable, not just to Airbnb, but also to the local authorities. Local authorities in this case include the resident HOAs. If you do the math and it doesn't add up, you are better off trying a different location.

Access to Popular Attractions

Naturally, properties that are closer to popular attractions experience more demand than those further away. Thus, it makes sense to charge higher for these properties. From tourists to business travelers, people generally want to be as close as possible to the places and activities they enjoy. Attractions like famous mountains, national parks, and museums have as much appeal to guests as beachfront properties.

People are naturally drawn to properties within close proximity to such attractions, so you can charge premium rates. You might also notice that these properties tend to have a higher occupancy rate than the alternatives, making them ideal for your investment journey. As a rule of thumb, you should strive to achieve as high an occupancy rate as possible, because this automatically translates to more rental income from the property.

Public Amenities and Facilities

Properties that are closer to facilities like gyms, restaurants, clubs, and shops fetch higher incomes than those further away. This is because such properties add a touch of convenience to guests during their stay. Instead of spending on an Uber or any other form of transportation for simple grocery shopping, guests can easily walk to their destination, saving on transportation costs.

On the same note, you'll also have a better chance of setting higher prices for properties that are closer to an elaborate transportation system. Easy access to public transport gives your guest the added benefit of coming to the property whenever they want. Where access to public amenities and facilities are concerned, convenience will always work to your advantage.

Seasonality

As you shop around for potential properties that suit your investment objectives, you should take a wider glance at the market in general. Identify the low and high seasons because this will directly affect your investment. Some areas have longer low seasons and short high seasons. This is something that many beginners never realize. If you invest in an area with longer low seasons, you'll be tying your money down unnecessarily. This is because you'll go through lengthy periods without earning a steady income.

Note that even during the low seasons, or when your property is vacant, you must still pay for cleaning and other utility bills to keep the property in good shape. In the long run, this property will drain your savings. On seasonality, consider properties in locations with high visitor traffic throughout the year, or at least most of the year. Such properties have a sustainably high demand for short-term rentals, so your investment will be safe.

As one of the key profitability factors in the Airbnb business or the wider real estate market in general, you should never take location for granted. Do your research, understand the location, get credible data, and use it to figure out the most ideal neighborhood for your investment.

Overseas Airbnb

Should you have Airbnbs out of the US?

Well, why not?

Airbnb is global, so if you feel you have what it takes, and have identified a promising market in another country, then go for it. Airbnb is one of those unique products that brought globalization to individual investors. More often, globalization is something we only see in corporations. Thanks to Airbnb, you can create your short-term rental empire in the US and beyond.

Now, while the prospect of going global sounds exciting, you have to approach it carefully, because there's just as much for you to lose as you can gain. All the ideas we've discussed in this book will apply in almost every other country you'd wish to diversify your investment into.

One of the most important things when setting up your Airbnb overseas is to ensure that you invest in a country and region with favorable laws and regulations. Naturally, you probably won't be in that country most of the time, so apart from the laws (which you have no control over), the other thing you should figure out is how to manage your property remotely (this is something you can control).

When setting up in another country, you'll have to think about how to communicate effectively with your guests, managing the check-in process, cleaning, repair, and maintenance, stocking up on supplies, and how to handle emergency situations. As you can see, your overseas Airbnb will have similar operational demands as your local Airbnb. This is why you need to implement a system that makes it easier to seamlessly run and manage your property. Let's look at some simple ideas that you can implement in your overseas Airbnb:

Property Automation

There are lots of property management systems in the market that can help with this. Property management systems help you keep everything organized from afar. With the right integration, you can automate everything from bookings to your calendar, cleaning, maintenance, and guest communication. Property automation helps you stay in control over day-to-day property management activities remotely.

Self-Check-ins

This is another interesting feature that your guests will appreciate. When turned on, guests don't have to contact you before checking in. A local key management service could be useful for this, helping you streamline guest entry and exit into your property. Alternatively, you could install a smart lock, key lockbox, or a digital keypad on the property.

Professional Cleaners

Since you won't be able to access the property physically, you need professional cleaners to keep things running smoothly. Look for a company with years of experience in the industry because you'll need professionals with flexible working hours. Guests don't always check out on time, so your cleaners must be able to maneuver such challenges and still offer the best cleaning experience with attention to detail.

To make their work easier, you could share a checklist of things or areas that they must never overlook, over and above their basic cleaning guide.

While most cleaners can take care of your laundry needs, not all cleaners do. If this is the case, look for a reliable laundry service, probably one that's as close to your property as possible. The faster you can get laundry cleaned and delivered, the better for you. Even with such a system in place, things don't always go according to plan. Therefore, invest in lots of spare linen to keep the house running in case of any delays from the laundry service. That way, you won't keep your cleaners waiting, and in return, they'll have your property ready for the next guest.

Maintenance Guide

Reliability is one of the most important things you need in a maintenance team. There are lots of tasks involved in maintaining an Airbnb to the standards you desire, and it will take a professional team to help you get that done. Your guests could need help with anything from gardening to plumbing and electrical works. It's good to know that you have a reliable team on standby.

Browse Airbnb support groups on social media to find some of the most recommended professionals in this field. If you can do it, you might also take a trip and visit the neighborhood in person. This gives you ample time to engage realtors and other professionals to learn more about the services they can offer you. Remember that as long as you own a short-term rental, it's always wise to spend a few days in the property to get a feel of what your guests live through. This informs you on what to improve or remove from the property to deliver a truly memorable experience.

Property Security

Security must always be a priority once you set up your Airbnb. This is even more important when managing your overseas property remotely. You'll need surveillance cameras outside your property. Security can be contentious, so you must find a good balance between protecting your property and assuring your guests of their security while on your property.

As a rule of thumb, you must abide by the local legislation and rules on security, especially if you intend to install CCTV cameras on the property. Installing cameras on your property should not infringe on your neighbor's rights to their privacy. Apart from that, you must also comply with Airbnb's policies on security installations. For example, hosts are prohibited from installing recording devices and hidden cameras in private areas within the property like bathrooms, bedrooms, and other guest living spaces.

Consider Co-Hosting

For remote property management, it might be useful to bring in a local co-host. A co-host generally assumes similar hosting responsibilities as they would in their own properties. Your co-host could be anyone from your friend, neighbor, or a professional co-host. Co-hosts help with pretty much all aspects of the hosting process, including meeting and greeting your guests, supervising cleaners and other handypersons, restocking supplies, and handling any other property management task that you might require.

Finally, running an overseas Airbnb remotely is an undertaking that requires your utmost attention to detail. Considering the distance problem, you'll have to be more hands-on with this investment whenever possible. By diversifying your investment portfolio to other countries, you enjoy the benefit of capitalizing on an even wider customer base. This, as far as your passive income goals are concerned, will be one of the smartest moves you make in this industry. Always remember that the laws that apply to Airbnb in the US won't necessarily apply in other countries, so make sure you understand the legal requirements to ensure you never run into problems with the local law.

Conclusion

Airbnb hasn't just challenged the way the hotel industry works, it has changed lives. Millions of hosts all over the world are closer to or have achieved financial independence through Airbnb. There's so much to learn, not just about Airbnb, but also from their business model, that can help you keep pushing towards your long-term financial goals.

While this book walks you through all the crucial information you need to set up your income-earner on Airbnb, we must also add a word of caution, that this is not an overnight-millionaire plan. This is a business like any other, and you must be prepared to do the work. It is more than a business, it is an investment. For that reason, it is a commitment to continuous improvement and upgrades, which will ultimately see you grow from your first listing to probably owning a portfolio of Airbnb properties.

Your investment in the Airbnb business is one of the smartest forms of gradual wealth creation you can come up with. It might not be an effortless process, but you will learn a lot about real estate investment and management in the process. This knowledge will ultimately become pivotal in establishing your investment portfolio.

In the course of managing your listing, you'll also interact with lots of professionals whose input will give you deeper insight into other services relevant to successfully managing your property, for example interior designers, cleaners, handypersons, contractors, and real estate agents. Ultimately, this is an extremely rewarding investment, and you'll derive much satisfaction in seeing your investment record multiple growth milestones.

While this book talks about Airbnb as the key to your financial freedom, you'll soon realize that there's more to financial freedom than the actual income you derive from short-term rentals. Financial freedom should also translate to getting more time to yourself. Most people struggle to create time in their lives because they are constantly engaged in various pursuits. Attaining financial freedom means making enough money to not have to worry about the things you were worried about when you were just starting out. This also means smart time management by delegating some duties to different people. Ultimately, financial freedom means a wholesome improvement in your standard of living. That's the Airbnb promise that many hosts have come to appreciate.

As you get into this business, it's common, especially for beginners, to pay more attention to the amount of money you'll make. While there's nothing wrong with that, this approach blinds you to the cost of making that money. Think about the costs in terms of time invested in the business, relationships that get strained over time, friendships, and so on. Time, for example, is one of the most precious commodities that you can never get back. A successful Airbnb business means setting up a reliable and steady source of passive income. At this point, you can comfortably step away from some of your daily pursuits and focus on spending more time with your loved ones. This, ultimately, is Airbnb's contribution to improving the quality of your life.

One of the most important lessons you should take from this book is the need to understand your market at all times. Market research is a never-ending task as long as your business is active. By its nature, Airbnb is a relationship business. You are catering to guests who seek a memorable stay on your property. Because of this personal nature, it's in your best interest to understand the market dynamics and trends so that you are in a better position to offer the best services to your customers.

Customer needs, tastes, and preferences change all the time, so your challenge will be trying to keep up. Some innovations move from additional services to necessities. For example, there was a time when self-check-ins were additional services that made your listing stand out. Today such services are considered necessities, or even the bare minimum in some markets. Guests won't be wowed by it, they'll expect it. Such is the importance of understanding the market, especially with respect to evolving customer needs.

At the beginning of this book, we highlighted the importance of convenience and comfort to your guests. Even as we wrap up this book, it's important to remind you of how weighty this issue is. Your guests' comfort and convenience are two factors that will be crucial to your success. From the furniture to the interior design and decor, do your best to ensure that guests check out of your property with nothing but good memories. At times it's simple things like adding more throw pillows, carpets, rugs, or runners that make guests feel so comfortable in your property.

Financial freedom doesn't necessarily mean having millions of dollars in your bank account. Having that much money would be great, of course, but what's even more important is being in a position where you have enough money to cater to your needs, your investments, savings, and plan for your future without ever worrying about what happens if your paycheck delays, or if you lose your job. Airbnb offers you the perfect platform to achieve this.

Finally, it's worth noting that there are more benefits to investing in Airbnb than the income angle. As your business grows, you'll come to appreciate the value of flexibility, freedom, and diversity as you restructure your time, work, and lifestyle in line with the demands of your investment.

Having read this book, you now have all the tools you need to make that first bold step into a new world of great opportunities and immense financial potential. Don't let anything or anyone hold you back. Go on and do great things. Push the limits, challenge the status quo and witness the immense financial transformation that will come into your life. I hope you enjoyed reading this book and found it quite valuable. Kindly leave a review on Amazon so other readers can similarly learn the tools to start their journey to financial freedom.

References

Agence France-Presse. (2018, July 5). Airbnb: the first 10 years—start-up to unicorn to US$30 billion business. *South China Morning Post.* https://www.scmp.com/lifestyle/travel-leisure/article/2153851/how-airbnb-founders-went-cash-strapped-roommates

Airbnb. (2021). Offer an easy check-in with the refreshed Trips tab. *Resource Center—Airbnb.* https://www.airbnb.com/resources/hosting-homes/a/offer-an-easy-check-in-with-the-refreshed-trips-tab-378

Airbnb. (2022, May 11). New and improved AirCover for hosts. *Resource Center—Airbnb.* https://www.airbnb.com/resources/hosting-homes/a/new-and-improved-aircover-for-hosts-469

Airbnb. (2023). Airbnb service fees. *Airbnb.* https://www.airbnb.com/help/article/1857

Airbnb. (2023). The Airbnb blog—belong anywhere. https://blog.atairbnb.com/

Airbnb. (2023). What regulations apply to my city? *Airbnb.* https://www.airbnb.com/help/article/961

Airbnb. (2023). Your local laws and taxes. *Airbnb.* https://www.airbnb.com/help/article/3029/

Alanna. (2020, October 30). 9 things to consider when investing in a STR. *The Distinguished Guest.* https://thedistinguishedguest.com/things-you-should-know-when-investing-buying-in-a-short-term-rental/

Ales, M. (2023). The importance of photography to your Airbnb listing. *Hometrack.* https://www.hometrack.net/blog/the-importance-of-photography-to-your-airbnb-listing#:~:text=Much%20like%20hiring%20a%20professional,increase%20in%20your%20nightly%20price.

Atkin, D. J. (2019, March 10). How Airbnb found its purpose and why it's a good one. *Medium.* https://medium.com/@douglas.atkin/how-airbnb-found-its-purpose-and-why-its-a-good-one-b5c987c0c216

Aydin, R. (2019, September 20). How 3 guys turned renting air mattresses in their apartment into a $31 billion company, Airbnb. *Business Insider.* https://www.businessinsider.com/how-airbnb-was-founded-a-visual-history-2016-2?r=US&IR=T

Barker, G. (2020, February 21). The Airbnb effect on housing and rent. *Forbes.* https://www.forbes.com/sites/garybarker/2020/02/21/the-airbnb-effect-on-housing-and-rent/?sh=52018f992226

BnB Specialist. (2022, December 26). *Bnb Specialist.* https://bnbspecialist.com/

Clifford, R. (2020, August 13). Competitors for Airbnb: Who's stealing market share from the industry giant? *Hospitable.* https://hospitable.com/competitors-for-airbnb/

Ditaranto, J. (2020, September 3). Everything to know about Airbnb Plus, including how listings are vetted, if they cost more, and if it's worth it. *Insider.* https://www.insider.com/guides/travel/what-is-airbnb-plus

Execs In The Know. (2022, April 21). Creating a world where anyone can belong anywhere. *Execs In The Know.* https://execsintheknow.com/magazines/april-2022-issue/creating-a-world-where-anyone-can-belong-anywhere/

GuestReady. (2022). How to get good Airbnb reviews. *GuestReady.* https://www.guestready.com/blog/how-to-get-good-airbnb-reviews/#:~:text=How%20to%20get%20good%20Airbnb%20reviews%201%20Be,ask%20guests%20to%20write%20you%20a%20review%20

Hostaway. (2015). 5 easy steps to starting an Airbnb. *Hostaway.* https://www.hostaway.com/5-easy-steps-to-starting-an-airbnb/

Hostaway. (2015). Furnishing your Airbnb: The complete guide. *Hostaway.* https://www.hostaway.com/furnishing-your-airbnb/

Hostfully. (2022, April 26). Become an expert: Airbnb pricing strategies. *Hostfully.* https://www.hostfully.com/blog/airbnb-pricing-strategies/#:~:text=Pricing%20is%20critical%20in%20realizing,your%20short%2Dterm%20rental%20business.

iGMS. (2021, June 1). Airbnb automation: 7 ways to put your business on autopilot. *iGMS.* https://www.igms.com/automate-airbnb/#:~:text=Airbnb%20automation%20is%20the%20process,%2C%20coordinating%20cleanings%2C%20and%20more.

Incfile. (n.d.). How to start an Airbnb. *Incfile.* https://www.incfile.com/start-a-business/airbnb

Elliot-McCrea, K. (2011, March 17). Airbnb was the breakout app at SxSW 2011. *Kellan Elliott-McCrea: Blog.* https://laughingmeme.org/2011/03/17/airbnb-was-the-breakout-app-at-sxsw-2011/

Lardinois, F. (2015, November 5). Expedia acquires Airbnb rival HomeAway for $3.9B. *TechCrunch.* https://techcrunch.com/2015/11/04/expedia-acquires-airbnb-rival-homeaway-for-3-9b

LearnBNB. (n.d.). Keys to long term success on Airbnb. *LearnBNB.* https://learnbnb.com/keys-to-long-term-success-on-airbnb/#:~:text=Keys%20to%20Long%20Term%20Success%20on%20Airbnb%201,%E2%80%93%20Listing%20and%20Reviews%20...%205%20Scale%20

LearnBNB. (n.d.). The ultimate beginner's guide to Airbnb hosting. *LearnBNB.* https://learnbnb.com/airbnb-hosting-beginners-guide/

LearnBNB. (n.d.). Airbnb dynamic pricing by hosts, for hosts. *LearnBNB.* https://learnbnb.com/dynamic-pricing-by-hosts-for-hosts/#more-43677

Marion. (2021, January 15). Airbnb's consistent rebrand focuses on the sense of belonging to a community. *The Branding Journal.* https://www.thebrandingjournal.com/2014/07/airbnbs-consistent-rebrand-focuses-sense-belonging-community/

Mohamed, T. (2020, December 11). A legendary venture-capitalist firm bought Airbnb shares for $0.01 each in 2009. *Markets Insider.* https://markets.businessinsider.com/news/stocks/airbnb-investor-sequoia-capital-bought-shares-1-cent-now-140-2020-12-1029885671

Mohammed, S. (2020, August 14). Airbnb, sustainable competitive advantage—Business strategy and the key success factors. *Medium.* https://shahmm.medium.com/airbnb-sustainable-competitive-advantage-business-strategy-and-the-key-success-factors-fe17eb9359d1

Neubauer, I. L. (2019, August 30). Countries that are cracking down on Airbnb. *The New Daily.* https://thenewdaily.com.au/life/travel/2019/08/30/countries-crack-down-airbnb/

PhotoAdKing. (2022, June 1). The case study: Booking.com—Tourism marketing. *PhotoADKing.* https://blog.photoadking.com/tourism-marketing-strategy-of-booking-com/

Price, L. (2022, September 6). How to start an Airbnb business. *Small Business Trends.* https://smallbiztrends.com/2021/11/how-to-start-an-airbnb-business.html

PRWeb. (2014, April 2). FlipKey experiences record growth; Now featuring more than 300,000 properties in 179 countries worldwide. *PRWeb.* https://www.prweb.com/releases/2014/04/prweb11724672.htm

Razinski, S. (2020, January 10). The definitive guide to starting an Airbnb business. *Ivetriedthat.* https://ivetriedthat.com/how-to-start-an-airbnb-business/#:~:text=Form%20a%20legal%20business%20entity%20to%20protect%20your,personal%20finances%20are%20separated%20from%20your%20business%20finances.

Rentals United. (2014). Airbnb competitors: Top 14 alternatives for property managers. *Rentals United.* https://rentalsunited.com/en/vacation-rental-guide/top-airbnb-competitors/

Rich, K. (n.d.). Earning money for travel with Airbnb. *The Blonde Abroad.* https://www.theblondeabroad.com/earning-money-for-travel-with-airbnb/

Rohde, J. (2022, February 23). What investors should know about STR real estate in 2022. *Roofstock.* https://learn.roofstock.com/blog/str-real-estate

Sarath. (2022, May 13). Top 100 Y combinator companies. *Eqvista.* https://eqvista.com/top-100-y-combinator-companies/

Scarlett, K. (2022, March 14). Short-term rental (STR) vs. long-term rental (LTR). *Greatdwellings.* https://www.greatdwellings.com/post/short-term-rental-vs-long-term-rental#:~:text=Long%2DTerm%20Rental%20(LTR),-Return%20to%20Blog

Shea, S. (2022, October 30). How to book Airbnb: Epic success in 8 easy steps! (2023). *The Broke Backpacker.* https://www.thebrokebackpacker.com/how-to-book-airbnb/#:~:text=Airbnb%20Booking%20Process%20%E2%80%93%20Tips%20and%20Tricks%201,essential%20to%20Airbnb%20reservation%20success.%20...%20More%20items

Singh, G. (2021, December 28). *Pixpa.* https://www.pixpa.com/blog/quotes-about-photography

Spillane, J. (2016, March 22). 4 keys to customer service that goes beyond the call of duty. *Business 2 Community.* https://www.business2community.com/brandviews/salesforce/4-keys-customer-service-goes-beyond-call-duty-01491001

Tatevosian, P. (2021, August 17). 3 competitive advantages Airbnb holds over hotels. *The Motley Fool.* https://www.fool.com/investing/2021/08/17/3-competitive-advantage-airbnb-holds-over-hotels/

Tom. (2022, June 24). Airbnb service fee: What you need to know. *Host Tools.* https://hosttools.com/blog/airbnb-rentals/what-you-need-to-know-about-the-airbnb-service-fee/

Wealth Insights. (2019, April 4). Expedia Group, Inc.: A long growth runway will fuel dividend growth. *Seeking Alpha*. https://seekingalpha.com/article/4252710-expedia-group-inc-long-growth-runway-will-fuel-dividend-growth

Whome. (n.d.). How to start an Airbnb with no money. *Whome Property Management*. https://whome.pt/blog/how-to-start-an-airbnb-with-no-money